W9-AIR-469

DISCERNING THE VOICE OF
GOD

How to Recognize When God Speaks

PRISCILLA SHIRER

LifeWay Press®
Nashville, Tennessee

Published by LifeWay Press®
©2006 • Priscilla Shirer
Fourth printing • December 2009

No part of this book may be reproduced or transmitted in any form or by any means, electronic or mechanical, including photocopying and recording, or by any information storage or retrieval system, except as may be expressly permitted in writing to Lifeway Press®; One Lifeway Plaza; Nashville, TN 37234-0175.

ISBN 978-1-4158-3662-0
Item 001315096

The book is a resource in the Bible Studies category of the Christian Growth Study Plan.
Course: CG-1229

Dewey Decimal Classification: 231.7
Subject Headings: GOD \ HOLY SPIRIT \ SPIRITUAL LIFE

All Scripture quotations, unless otherwise indicated, are taken from the New American Standard Bible®, Copyright ©1960, 1962, 1968, 1971, 1972, 1975, 1977, 1995 by the Lockman Foundation. Used by permission. (*www.lockman.org*)
Scripture quotations marked NLT are taken from the Holy Bible, New Living Translation, copyright ©1996. Used by permission of Tyndale House Publishers, Inc., Wheaton, IL 60189 USA. All rights reserved.
Scripture quotations marked HCSB are taken from the Holman Christian Standard Bible®, copyright ©1999, 2000, 2001, 2002 by Holman Bible Publishers. Used by permission.
Scripture quotations marked AMP are taken from The Amplified® Bible, copyright ©1954, 1958, 1962, 1964, 1965, 1987 by The Lockman Foundation. Used by permission. (*www.lockman.org*)
Scripture quotations marked NIV are taken from the Holy Bible, New International Version, copyright ©1973, 1978, 1984 by International Bible Society.
Scripture quotations marked *The Message* are from THE MESSAGE. Copyright © by Eugene H. Peterson, 1993, 1994, 1995. Used by permission of NavPress Publishing Group.
Scripture quotations marked RSV are from the Revised Standard Version of the Bible, copyright 1946, 1952, © 1971, 1973 by the National Council of the Churches of Christ in the U.S.A., and used by permission.

To order additional copies of this resource: WRITE LifeWay Christian Resources Customer Service; One LifeWay Plaza; Nashville, TN 37234-0133; FAX order to (615) 251-5933; PHONE (800) 458-2772; ORDER ONLINE at *www.lifeway.com*; E-MAIL *orderentry@lifeway.com*; or VISIT the LifeWay Christian Store serving you.

Printed in the United States of America

Leadership and Adult Publishing
LifeWay Church Resources
One LifeWay Plaza
Nashville, TN 37234-0175

CONTENTS

⌒⌒ ABOUT THE AUTHOR ⌒⌒

 Priscilla Shirer is a Bible teacher whose ministry is focused on the expository teaching of the Word of God to women. Her desire is to see women not only know the uncompromising truths of Scripture intellectually but experience them practically by the power of the Holy Spirit. Priscilla is a graduate of the Dallas Theological Seminary with a Master's degree in Biblical Studies. For over a decade she has been a conference speaker for major corporations, organizations, and Christian audiences across the United States and the world.

Priscilla is now in full-time ministry to women. She is the author of *A Jewel in His Crown, A Jewel in His Crown Journal, And We Are Changed: Transforming Encounters with God,* and *He Speaks to Me: Preparing to Hear from God.*

Priscilla is the daughter of pastor, speaker, and well-known author Dr. Tony Evans. She is married to her best friend, Jerry. The couple resides in Dallas with their two young sons, Jackson and Jerry Jr.

Jerry and Priscilla have founded Going Beyond Ministries where they are committed to seeing believers receive the most out of their relationship with the Lord.

⌒⌒ ABOUT THE STUDY ⌒⌒

Welcome to *Discerning the Voice of God!* The material in this book is divided into five days of individual study and one small-group session each week when you will process with others what you have studied. The small-group sessions provide an excellent opportunity to share what the Lord is teaching you as well as learn from what the Lord is teaching other women in your group.

Each day of individual study will take about 30 minutes. The learning activities provide a time of application and reflection. These things may also be topics of discussion in your small group. I strongly encourage you to complete all the learning activities to get the most from your study. Throughout the study you will also see flower icons followed by fill-in-the-blank statements. These are the key principles for each day. Pay special attention to these—they are designed to reinforce the message of the material you are studying.

As a part of my preparation for this Bible study, I had the opportunity to ask many godly people to complete this thought: "I know the Lord is speaking to me when ..." You will find their comments at the beginning of many of your daily lessons.

You may want to keep a notebook or journal close by to jot down thoughts the Holy Spirit reveals to you as you study. There are some activities throughout the study that will instruct you to answer on a separate sheet of paper. You may want to put those in your journal as well.

As you commit to this study, ask the Holy Spirit for guidance as you seek to better prepare yourself to recognize God's voice.

∽INTRODUCTION ∽

Welcome! I am a believer in Jesus Christ. He was sent to earth to die because the Father so passionately loved me that He couldn't bear to live without me. I have spent most of my Christian life leaning on this belief without really experiencing it.

I was taught that a relationship with God was a personal one in which God speaks to His children. I sat in many prayer meetings where passionate believers shared stirring encounters with God's voice while my own soul was filled with overwhelming confusion. How did these saints know God was speaking?

I made a decision to believe God speaks but not disappoint myself by believing He would speak to me. I hid my growing dissatisfaction with my Bible study and a powerless prayer time. I thought this was the way it would always be, until the day God spoke personally and intimately to me. An encounter with His presence made me different: I was filled with a hunger for the presence of God and fully convinced that the goal of my ministry should be to whet the appetites of others for the same. In your hands you hold a piece of my passion.

Discerning the voice of God is a divine mystery because it is a supernatural work the Holy Spirit does in us. This study cannot give you a formula by which you can discern His voice with 100 percent accuracy. As you practice discerning, know God graciously allows our errors to be the best teacher in hearing correctly in the future.

These next pages will guide you through six weeks of study. The first week will challenge your level of anticipation to hear from God. The second and third weeks will look in-depth at the Holy Spirit as God's primary method of leading His children. The fourth and fifth weeks will cover the nature of God's voice which reveals His character and His purposes. And finally, week six will examine Abraham's illustration of what our response should be when God speaks. I am praying you will be challenged and emerge from this study better equipped to hear the magnificent voice of our great God.

Open your heart completely to what the Spirit wants to teach you and the way He wants to teach it. Ask the Lord to break through the barriers. He is God and can do whatever He wants to get His word to you. As I prepared for this project, God began to infiltrate my cozy Christianity with His unconventional methods and I have emerged better for it. The more ways we can hear God speak, the more we will hear!

Blessings,

Priscilla

Lord, heighten my spiritual senses to

see that which is not visible

hear that which is not audible

sense that which is not tangible

believe that which is unbelievable.

Teach me to sort through

the noises of this world to

hear and discern Your powerful,

wonderful, pure, precious voice.

ANTICIPATING THE VOICE OF GOD

My sheep hear My voice, I know them, and they follow Me. John 10:27, HCSB

1. Jesus was clear to point out a _____, naming us His _____:

"My sheep …"

Romans 8:16—*The Spirit Himself testifies together with our spirit that we are*

_____ _____.

2. Jesus points out not only a _____ but a _____ of being His sheep:

" … hear My voice."

John 8:47—*The one who is from God _____ God's words.*

3. Jesus points out a _____, a _____ and also

a _____ for being His sheep:

"I know My sheep."

_____ is the foundation for getting to know God.

4. Jesus points out a _____, a _____,

a _____, and also a _____ from His sheep:

"They follow Me."

John 10:11—*I am the _____ shepherd. The good shepherd lays down His life for the sheep.*

Hebrews 13:20-21— *Now may the God of peace … the _____ Shepherd of the sheep—*

with the blood of the everlasting covenant, equip you with all that is good to do His will.

Anticipating the Voice of God

Day 1   EXPECT TO HEAR IT

HE SPEAKS

I will stand on my guard post And station myself on the rampart; And I will keep watch to see what He will speak to me. Habakkuk 2:1

Call to Me, and I will answer you, and I will tell you great and mighty things, which you do not know. Jeremiah 33:3

GOD WILL SPEAK TO THE HEARTS *of those who prepare themselves to hear; and conversely, those who do not so prepare themselves will hear nothing even though the Word of God is falling upon their outer ears every Sunday.[1] —A.W. Tozer*

I spent much of my Christian life not hearing God. I had read about how He spoke to people in the Bible, and even about modern-day believers who had an intimacy with Him that allowed them to hear His voice. But I rarely, if ever, experienced that type of connection with God. My relationship with Him was more one-sided. In prayer, I talked and He listened. I approached my Bible reading as an opportunity to learn about God, while never anticipating and expecting that the God of the universe would really speak to me about the personal details of my life.

Then my Bible study took me to Habakkuk, and I read about a man who desperately needed to hear from God and was amazingly confident that He would indeed answer. God shattered the season of divine silence in my life by convicting me about my lack of expectancy and anticipation to hear from Him. This is where clear communication with God begins: with a believer approaching her relationship to God and His Word with anticipation, expecting Him to speak.

Clear communication with God begins when I _____ God and His Word with _____, expecting Him to speak.

If you have experienced a time when your prayers seemed unheard, how did you feel toward God?

_____

Did this instance cause you to doubt that God desires to speak to you? ○ yes ○ no   If so, why?

_____

Deuteronomy 5:31
As for you, stand here by Me, that I may speak to you.

Micah 7:7, NLT
My God will certainly hear me.

Throughout Scripture God paints a picture of His relationship with His beloved as one in which He responds and speaks. Believers in the Bible didn't call to God and then walk away despondent because they assumed God wouldn't respond. They looked expectantly and eagerly for the response God would offer.

Many of us don't really believe God will speak to us and give us specific directions concerning the details of our lives. We claim to believe that God speaks, but we are secretly discouraged because we don't see evidence of His voice in our lives. We need to approach the Father with an expectancy that He will speak.

Approach the Father with an expectancy that He will speak.

THE STORY OF HABAKKUK

Habakkuk desperately needed to hear from God. He saw the continued iniquity and destruction of Judah and called out to God for help. Initially, it appeared that God wasn't answering or hearing, yet Habakkuk never considered that he wouldn't receive divine instruction.

On the inside of the front or back cover of this book, make a list of personal circumstances troubling you. As you work through this Bible study, focus on these circumstances and how God is speaking to you concerning them.

In Habakkuk 1:2-3, the discouraged prophet asked two questions of God: "How long?" (v. 2) and "Why?" (v. 3). These questions probably strike a chord with you as well. When the circumstances of life seem to be closing in on us and we see no end in sight, we want to know how long we will have to continue calling out to God with seemingly no response. We also want to know why He would continue to allow the circumstances we face.

Think of a request you have been bringing to the Lord for a long time. Do you still expect God to respond and speak to you, or are you losing hope? Write your thoughts below.

_____

_____

Habakkuk 1:5
Look among the nations! Observe! Be astonished! Wonder! Because I am doing something in your days— You would not believe if you were told.

We don't know how long Habakkuk had been calling out to God, but when it appeared that He was not answering, Habakkuk pointed an accusatory finger at God. Open your Bible and read his prayer in Habakkuk 1:2-4. Habakkuk became increasingly discouraged and started to lose confidence that the Lord would answer him. God finally spoke up and answered the prophet in verse 5.

Read this verse in the margin and underline the actions God commanded Habakkuk to take.

With these words, God gave Habakkuk spiritual vision. The prophet received encouragement to look around and observe. While Habakkuk waited on God to answer, God was already answering! God wanted to restore Habakkuk's confidence by showing him that He was not idle and uninterested in the demise of Judah. Even though the prophet wasn't seeing God respond in the way and timing he expected, God was speaking and moving. He always is—even in His silence.

Throughout the next week ask the Lord for spiritual vision concerning each of the personal circumstances you listed earlier. Take deliberate time to see God's handiwork in each situation.

Proverbs 3:5-6
Trust in the LORD with all your heart And do not lean on your own understanding. In all your ways acknowledge Him, And He will make your paths straight.

CONFIDENCE RESTORED

With his eyes newly opened, Habakkuk was able to rebuild his confidence in God's ability and sovereignty. Instead of making his request by shaking an accusing finger at God, Habakkuk chose words that revealed his expectation and anticipation.

Read Habakkuk 1:12-13. On a separate sheet of paper, make a list of the attributes of God mentioned in these verses. Use these words to write a short prayer expressing your confidence in God's control of your circumstances and desire to speak to you regarding them. Put this page in a place where you can see it often.

Habakkuk's second prayer is completely different from his first. After seeing his circumstances through new eyes, his level of anticipation increased.

Which prayer of Habakkuk's reflects your current feelings about hearing God's voice? Mark where you are on the continuum.

first prayer (vv. 2-3)   second prayer (vv. 12-13)
doubtful and accusatory   expectant and confident

Not until Habakkuk's approach to God changed from doubtful to confident and expectant did he begin to receive directions from God as to what he should do. Initially, God spoke to prove that He was indeed up to something and to build Habakkuk's confidence, but the second time He spoke to give instructions and guidance. Could your level of expectancy be a factor in how clearly and frequently you hear God's voice?

If we come to Him doubting His ability to speak, we will have a difficult time listening. So we must come expectantly.[2]
—Charles Stanley

What has the Holy Spirit taught you as you studied today?

_____

_____

_____

Psalm 5:3
In the morning, O LORD, You will hear my voice; In the morning I will order my prayer to You and eagerly watch.

What is God asking you to do as a result of today's study?

_____

_____

_____

Write a prayer responding to God's commands to you.

_____

_____

_____

_____

1. A. W. Tozer, *The Root of Righteousness: Tapping the Bedrock of True Spirituality* (Camp Hill, PA: Christian Publications, 1986), 21.
2. Charles Stanley, *How to Know God's Will* (Colorado Springs: NavPress, 1989), 12.

Day 2   WAIT PATIENTLY FOR IT

HE SPEAKS
The vision is yet for the appointed time …
Though it tarries, wait for it;
For it will certainly come, it will not delay.
Habakkuk 2:3

IF YOU WANT TO HEAR GOD'S *voice clearly and you are uncertain, then remain in His presence until He changes this uncertainty. Often much can happen during this waiting for the Lord. Sometimes He changes pride into humility; doubt into faith and peace; sometimes lust into purity. The Lord can and will do it.*[1]
—*Corrie Ten Boom*

One thing I learned from my friend and mentor Anne Graham Lotz is God *does* speak to His children. She once said to me, "I never make a major decision, especially one that will affect another person, before I receive direction from God." For every major ministry decision she has made, she can pinpoint a specific Scripture verse as the one God used to personally direct that decision. Anne so anticipates and expects an answer from God that she is resolved to wait on Him for guidance before coming to a final decision on a matter.

Recall a time when you acted *before* hearing from God.
What happened? Share your experience with your small group.

Psalm 27:14
Wait for the LORD;
Be strong, and let your heart take courage;
Yes, wait for the LORD.

_____

_____

The process of waiting for a message from God can be just as important as the message itself. In waiting, my faith and intimacy with the Lord grow. Often something I learn while waiting prepares me for the message so that I am not as surprised by it as I might have been otherwise; thus, I am more willing to obey.

 **The process of** _____ **for a message from God**

is just as important as the _____ **itself.**

If we approach our relationship to God and His Word expecting Him to speak, we will be more patient because we know He will come through in His time. Just like the rest of us, Habakkuk had to wait for God's Word and its fulfillment.

WAITING ON HIS WORD

We are always willing to wait on things that are important to us. We will stay by our phones awaiting a call regarding a career opportunity or a report from the doctor's office. We will wait in line for much-needed groceries. We will wait out the long months before the arrival of a baby. The value we place on an object or person dictates the amount of time we are willing to wait on them. The importance of hearing God's voice was paramount to Habakkuk.

Look up Habakkuk 2:1 and write it in your own words in the margin.

The Hebrew word for *stand* is *amad*. It means "to endure, remain and to be standing both in body and attitude." The Hebrew word for *station* is *yatsab*. It means "to take one's stand." Habakkuk's usage of these two words shows how seriously he expected God to answer and how determined he was to wait on that answer. He didn't seek to fill his void with any alternatives. He just waited on God—posture militant, stance strong, and resolve sure. He was on the lookout for an answer.

Which of the following adjectives describe your stance when waiting on God's Word to you? Check all that apply.
- ⃝ wavering ⃝ confident ⃝ critical
- ⃝ doubtful ⃝ nonchalant ⃝ other _____

In Habakkuk's day a watchman would minimize all distractions to concentrate fully on the task of protecting the city from approaching enemies. The guard would not allow anyone to coerce him from his post. Likewise, the prophet wasn't gong to make a move until he received divine direction. If we value God's Word as Habakkuk did, we should be willing to wait patiently and not move until we have received it.

Habakkuk described where he would wait: "on the watchtower." The watchtower was positioned well above the ground to provide a broad view for miles around. It gave the guard in the tower a different view of his circumstances by placing him high above ground level. Habakkuk purposed to remove himself from the depression and anxiety of his ground-level circumstances and get above them. He took his eyes off his circumstances and watched only for God.

Look back at the list you made inside the front or back cover of this book. Place a plus sign beside the ones in which you are patiently waiting to hear from God and a minus sign beside the ones in which you have taken action before hearing from Him.

If you told God on your knees that you had reached an impasse and … were handing it over to him, then leave it with him. Do not go to the first Christian you meet and say, "You know, I have an awful problem; I don't know what to do." Don't discuss it. Leave it with God, and go on the watch-tower.[2]
—D. Martyn Lloyd-Jones

❊ WAITING ON FULFILLMENT OF HIS WORD ❊

We often want to immediately run ahead the moment we hear God's leading and direction. Instead of walking in daily obedience, we desire to see the end result of God's plan instantly.

Habakkuk 2:3
The vision is yet for the appointed time; It hastens toward the goal, and it will not fail. Though it tarries, wait for it; For it will certainly come, it will not delay.

When God began to give Habakkuk the guidance he had been seeking, He buffered it with the words recorded in Habakkuk 2:3 (in margin). Habakkuk's need for patience was so great, the Lord prefaced His message with a reminder for Habakkuk to not try to carry out God's plan before its due season.

God encouraged Habakkuk to be patient by assuring him of four specific promises regarding the vision He was about to reveal. Underline them in the margin (Hab. 2:3).

In the Book of Genesis, Abraham and Sarah faced a situation where they were forced to wait on God. What was the Lord's promise to Abraham and Sarah in Genesis 18:9-18?

According to Genesis 21:1-2 when did God accomplish what He had spoken to Abraham and Sarah?

---

2 Peter 3:9
The Lord is not slow about His promise.

How had Sarah and Abraham impatiently tried to fulfill God's promise of offspring (Gen. 16:1-4)?

Don't flounder when time passes as you wait to see God's promises fulfilled. Stand firm and walk in daily obedience to God.

Great relief awaits those asking God to provide a mate, financial assistance, a ministry opportunity, career advancement, or simply His direction. We can be free from the burden of trying to make things happen when we know He promises to fulfill His own Word. God told Habakkuk what he would need to walk in patience before the Lord.

On what must the righteous depend? (Hab. 2:4) _____

While the righteous man trusts God will fulfill His Word, the proud man (self-reliant) depends on himself to bring things to pass. When we seek God in faith, He promises us great reward (see Heb. 11:6).

What has the Holy Spirit taught you as you studied today?

_____

_____

What is God asking you to do as a result of today's study?

_____

_____

Write a prayer responding to God's commands to you.

_____

_____

_____

1. Corrie Ten Boom, *Not I, but Christ* (Nashville: Thomas Nelson Publishers, 1984), 24.
2. D. Martyn Lloyd-Jones, *Faith Tried and Triumphant* (Grand Rapids: Baker, 1996), 28.

Day 3 PLAN TO OBEY IT

HIS LEADING IS ONLY FOR *those who are already committed to do as He may choose. To such it may be said: "God is able to speak loud enough to make a willing soul hear."*[1]
—*Lewis Sperry Chafer*

HE SPEAKS
If you will indeed obey My voice and keep My covenant, then you shall be My own possession among all the peoples, for all the earth is Mine.
Exodus 19:5

Several weeks ago, I asked my husband which pair of shoes looked best with my outfit. I knew which pair I was going to wear regardless of his response. When I chose my option instead of his, he was understandably irritated. These days when I ask for his opinion he is hesitant to give a response. Instead he just says, "Why are you asking me? You're going to do what you want to do anyway!"

I wonder how often we ask God for His opinion while knowing full well we plan to stick with our own plan. Yes, we will follow Him, but only when and if His prescription will be comfortable to follow and will closely match our own desires. If we want to keep the lines of communication open and flourishing, we must prepare to abandon our plans when they don't coincide with His. Obedience is the key to hearing His still, small voice.

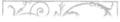 _____ **is the key to hearing His still, small voice.**

Luke 8:18, NLT
Be sure to pay attention to what you hear. To those who are open to my teaching, more understanding will be given. But to those who are not listening, even what they think they have will be taken away from them.

Do you normally consider what your response will be to God before you seek His direction? ○ yes ○ no

OBEDIENCE NO MATTER WHAT

Habakkuk wasn't just passionate about hearing God's direction. He also was serious about fully accepting God's commands no matter what they were. He thought ahead and planned to respond in obedience.

"I will stand on my guard post and station myself on the rampart; and I will keep watch to see what He will speak to me, and how I may reply when I am reproved" (Hab. 2:1).

Strong's defines the word *reprove* in Habakkuk 2:1 as "rebuke, correction, reproof, refutation, chastened."[3]

What does Habakkuk's use of the word imply about the type of response he expected from God?

_____

_____

If we settle ahead of time that we will obey whatever God tells us, we will go into our time with him ready to hear his voice.[2]
—Henry and Richard Blackaby

Habakkuk seemed to think that whatever God said, at least part of it would be a rebuke to him; but he was willing to accept even God's harsh words.

How do you usually respond to God's Word even when it may be something you do not want to hear? Rank your responses 1 (the response you most frequently use) through 4 (the response you least frequently use).

_____ ignore—act like I never heard it

_____ consider—weigh my options

_____ obey—follow His directions regardless of how I feel

_____ keep praying—hope God will change His response

Read the passages listed below and match them to God's response to people who do not obey His Word.

Jeremiah 6:16-19	sent a famine of His Word
Amos 8:9-11	refused to listen
Zechariah 7:12-13	brought disaster to the people

To know God's Word and not obey it is sin against Him. Sin reaps consequences. One consequence is that we will hear His voice far less frequently. As we blatantly ignore and disobey God, we build a callous around our spiritual ears so that we don't hear the voice of God. He knows if we are pure in our desire to do what He says. Matthew 5:8 extends a promise to the pure in heart: "They shall see God."

Moses was a man who knew God intimately. God separated His relationship with Moses from any other man of the day when He said He spoke to him "face to face" as a man speaks to his friend (see Num. 12). But Moses was far from perfect. He was a murderer (see Ex. 2:12) and had once tried to shirk God's responsibility for him (see Ex. 4:13). But God still used him and spoke to him. He gives the reason why in Deuteronomy 5:29-31 (in margin).

True blessing isn't just found in hearing God's voice but in heeding it. When we obey, no matter how unusual His instructions may be, we create a solid foundation on which God can display His supernatural activity in our lives.

Recently, my youngest son, Jerry, was ill. I kept waking up as he wheezed and coughed. At 4:00 a.m. I was awakened not by coughing but by the Spirit of God. He encouraged me to go to the nursery, lay a hand on my son, and pray for his healing. I debated for at least 10 minutes. I had just gotten back in bed and didn't feel like going all the way back up those stairs. Could it be the supernatural intervention God had planned with my son's health hinged on whether or not I would obediently follow His simple instructions? I got up and went to Jerry's room. I laid my hands on him and prayed for God's healing. I poured Scriptures over him. Afterward I went back downstairs. He slept soundly the rest of the night.

The next morning my husband asked if I had given Jerry medicine in the middle of the night. I told him I hadn't. He said, "After you went up there, the coughing stopped. I thought you must have given him something." I said, "Yes, I gave him something all right! God's healing!"

Many times God has asked me to do something I thought was too crazy to consider. Yet in ignoring His leading, have I often missed out on the supernatural and glorious results He had planned if I had just obeyed His instructions?

I wonder what supernatural rewards and divine interventions are awaiting us if we plan beforehand to fully obey when God speaks?

Deuteronomy 5:29-31
Oh that they had such a heart in them [like Moses], that they would fear Me, and keep all My commandments ... Go, say to them, "Return to your tents." But as for you [Moses] stand here by Me, that I may speak to you.

Psalm 19:11
In keeping the [word of the Lord] there is great reward.

Isaiah 48:18, HCSB
If only you had paid attention to My commands. Then your peace would have been like a river, and your righteousness like the waves of the sea.

Matthew 7:24, NIV
Everyone who hears these words of mine and puts them into practice is like a wise man.

What has the Holy Spirit taught you as you studied today?

_____

_____

What is God asking you to do as a result of today's study?

_____

_____

Write a prayer responding to God's commands to you.

_____

_____

_____

_____

1. Lewis Sperry Chafer, *He That Is Spiritual* (Findlay, OH: Dunham Publishing, 1918), 114.
2. Henry and Richard Blackaby, *Hearing God's Voice* (Nashville: Broadman and Holman, 2002), 245.
3. James Strong, *The Exhaustive Concordance of the Bible* (Nashville: Holman Bible Publishers, n.d.), 123.

Day 4 LISTEN FOR IT

HE SPEAKS
As you enter the house of God, keep your ears open and your mouth shut! ... he is in heaven, and you are only here on earth. So let your words be few.
Ecclesiastes 5:1-2, NLT

THINGS DON'T CHANGE *when I talk to God; things change when God talks to me.*[1] —*Bob Sorge*

Listening for the voice of God seems to be a misplaced phenomenon. Lost in the midst of busyness and growing religious activity is the art of being still—consciously and deliberately tuning our ears to hear God.

Could it be we don't hear God because we have trained ourselves not to hear Him? Our busy lifestyles have squelched out the clear, powerful voice of God so we no longer even recognize it. We must carve out time to purposefully listen for God's voice through prayer, meditation on His Word, and worship. If we listen we'll hear the voice that speaks eternally.

🌸 **I must carve out time to purposefully listen for God's voice through**

_____, _____ **on His Word**

and _____.

According to our main Scripture today, we should "let [our] words be few" (Eccl. 5:2). This implies that our time listening should outweigh our time talking. I'm not saying we shouldn't voice our needs, requests, and desires to God, but we shouldn't allow these things to keep us from hearing what He wants to say.

> Scripture repeats the pattern of God calling His people away from action to stillness. Underline the words that indicate this in the Scriptures in the margin.

> Circle the phrases in Ecclesiastes 5:1-2 and Habakkuk 2:20 that reveal the *reason* for silence, and put a box around the phrases in Psalm 46:10 and Isaiah 30:15 that explain the *result* of silence.

TWO TYPES OF LISTENING

There are two types of listening—*passive listening* and *aggressive listening*. We engage in passive listening most frequently. We hear with our physical ears, but we don't digest the truth of what is being said. God wants aggressive listeners who look intently at His Word and listen deliberately to what He has to say.

Although it's easiest to concentrate on listening to God during times of prayer, meditation, and worship, we can aggressively listen at other times. I practice listening while I am doing all sorts of mundane tasks. I purposefully focus on God, invite the Holy Spirit to speak, and concentrate my attention on Him.

> Make a list of everyday tasks you will accomplish today. How can you turn them into opportunities to aggressively listen for God to speak?

Task   *How I can aggressively listen*

_____   _____

_____   _____

_____   _____

_____   _____

Ecclesiastes 5:1-2, NLT
As you enter the house of God, keep your ears open and your mouth shut! … he is in heaven, and you are only here on earth. So let your words be few.

Habakkuk 2:20
The LORD is in His holy temple. Let all the earth be silent before Him.

Psalm 46:10, NIV
Be still, and know that I am God.

Isaiah 30:15
The Lord GOD, the Holy One of Israel, has said, "In repentance and rest you will be saved, In quietness and trust is your strength."

James 1:25
*The one who looks
intently at the
perfect law, the
law of liberty, and
abides by it, not
having become a
forgetful hearer but
an effectual doer,
this [woman] shall
be blessed in what
[she] does.*

For most of my Christian life, I left my prayer time feeling like I just had a one-way conversation and received absolutely no response. I desperately longed to have a regular encounter with God. I believed God wanted more out of my prayer life with Him and so did I. That's when I began to take seriously the art of listening, making prayer more about God and less about me.

Stephen Verney suggests that there are three stages of listening prayer or contemplation: "First, 'it is me and him.' I come to prayer conscious of myself, my need, my desires. I pour these out to God. Second, prayer becomes 'him and me.' Gradually, I become more conscious of the presence of God than of myself. 'Then it is only him.' God's presence arrests me, captivates me, warms me, works on me."[2]

Listening to God involves your participation. You must engage your body, mind, and spirit. In her book *The Joy of Listening to God*, Joyce Huggett describes this experience: "I closed my eyes to shut out visual stimuli … I closed my ears … by dealing authoritatively with the distractions which threatened my ability to tune in to God. … I closed a series of shutters on the surface level of my life, thus holding at bay hindrances to hearing the still, small voice of God."[3]

> List on a separate sheet of paper the "visual stimuli" that normally distract you from tuning in to God. Go back and list conscious efforts you can make to remove those distractions.

I am leery of giving you a formula to follow when spending time listening to God. For each person this experience will be different. The Lord wants to deal with you as an individual. Just as intimacy between a man and a woman doesn't need to be prescribed down to the last detail, neither does your intimate time with the Lord. God clearly speaks to His children, however, when they pray, meditate on His Word, and worship Him.

PRAYER

In 1 Corinthians 14:15, the Apostle Paul said he prayed with his mind and also with his spirit. Mental prayer is what we participate in most often, but we shouldn't limit our prayer lives to it. In praying with my mind, I work through my prayer list. I ask for forgiveness of sins, offer Him thanks for specific things, bring Him needs for which I desire His intervention, and intercede on behalf of others. Instead of ending my prayer time when my list is complete, I wait and quiet my mind so I can move to a Spirit-led time of prayer. I believe this is, at least in part, what Paul referred to in his letter.

> Read 1 Corinthians 2:10-12 in your Bible. According to this passage, why do we need to connect with the Spirit during prayer? Write your answer in the margin.

Spirit-led prayer gives the Holy Spirit an opportunity to direct our prayer time. He alone knows the thoughts of God and can express them as He leads us in prayer. When I embark on this journey in my prayer time, I turn my thoughts inward and allow the Holy Spirit to direct my time in prayer. He brings to mind people or situations about which I might not normally think. He causes me to recall sins I didn't realize or had forgotten I committed. He brings a specific verse to my mind. I am often directed to worship God for a specific characteristic or attribute. The more I practice this type of prayer, the more I develop the ability to do it anywhere, no matter the chaos swirling around me.

Joshua 1:8,
THE MESSAGE
Don't for a minute let this Book of The Revelation be out of mind. Ponder and meditate on it day and night.

MEDITATION

Over and over the Scripture points believers to meditation. Some of the most precious times I have with God come not during a corporate worship experience but during a time of personal meditation. During this time in my "secret place" with God I normally just sit still in God's presence, sometimes in silence, with a specific Bible verse on my mind.

Psalm 77:12
I will meditate on all Your work And muse on Your deeds.

Meditation is a discipline because it requires you to control your desire to fill the silence with activity. You just sit, think, and ponder; you may concentrate on Scripture, the goodness of God to you, or the goodness of God Himself.

My Bible and journal are my only companions during this time. I write down the thoughts the Holy Spirit brings to my mind and record the messages I sense the Lord leading me to hear from Him.

Psalm 119:15
I will meditate on Your precepts And regard Your ways.

> Stop now for a short time of meditation. Turn to Isaiah 50:4-5 and read it slowly and personally. Put your name into the verse as you read it, and record in your journal or on a separate sheet of paper any thoughts the Lord brings to mind as you meditate.

WORSHIP

Meditation often leads to spontaneous worship. Many times I will use praise and worship music as the backdrop for my time with God. As the worship music speaks of His attributes, I ponder the lyrics and allow them to lead me into personal worship. During this time, God leads me and shows me how He wants to be worshiped and how I should spend my time with Him. As the music envelops me, I am both overwhelmed and encouraged by an awareness of His presence.

As I sit, I begin to hear God—not always with specific instructions, but with a sense of His presence guiding, leading, and pursuing me wholeheartedly. I sense that He is with me and near me and the words of the passage on which I am meditating come alive.

By listening to God through prayer, meditation on His Word, and worship, the Holy Spirit will begin to speak to you, revealing God's personal and timely word for your life.

What has the Holy Spirit taught you as you studied today?

_____

_____

_____

_____

What is God asking you to do as a result of today's study?

_____

_____

_____

_____

Write a prayer responding to God's commands to you.

_____

_____

_____

_____

---

1. Bob Sorge, *Secrets of the Secret Place: Keys to Igniting Your Personal Time with God* (Lee's Summit, MO: Oasis House, 2005), 11.
2. Joyce Huggett, *The Joy of Listening to God: Hearing the Many Ways God Speaks to Us* (Downers Grove, IL; InterVarsity Press, 1986), 65.
3. Ibid., 53.

Day 5   HAVE FAITH IN IT

I KNOW THE LORD IS SPEAKING TO ME *when the voice I hear is always challenging, always convicting, and never allows me to be comfortable where I am. Not having a father, what an honor it is to have One who loves me so much that His greatest desire is to see me grow.* —Kirk Franklin

HE SPEAKS
The word they heard did not profit them, because it was not united by faith in those who heard.
Hebrews 4:2

Over this past week we have looked at the importance of expecting God to speak in a clear and personal way. That belief is paramount to experiencing communication with God. Today we will look at a final key component in preparing ourselves to discern God's voice: faith in the power of the Word.

In 2004, I was facing a very specific issue of healing. As I searched for a solution from doctors, the Holy Spirit convicted me that I had sought an answer from everyone except the Lord. I had not asked Him to heal me. I had asked for advice and medication from doctors, sought guidance from Web sites and books, but still had not verbalized my request to the Lord.

As I searched my heart, I realized the reason I hadn't prayed about it was that I didn't truly expect the Lord to answer me. I read and believed the miracles of the New Testament and had even seen and heard of Him healing modern-day believers, but in the deep recesses of my heart I didn't believe He would do it for me.

Hebrews 10:22
Let us draw near with a sincere heart in full assurance of faith, having our hearts sprinkled clean from an evil conscience and our bodies washed with pure water.

Carefully examine the paragraph above. Exactly what did my lack of faith prevent?
O God from healing me
O me from taking my problem to God
O God from doing what I told Him to do

Faith as small as a mustard seed is enough to come to God for His power (see Matt. 17:20). My lack of faith in God's desire to speak to my current situation didn't keep God from acting. It kept me from asking. Therefore, I didn't hear God's voice and receive His direction. Faith in God's Word is the final component necessary to hear from God and clearly discern His voice.

_____ **in God's Word is necessary to hear from God and clearly discern His voice.**

Are you facing a specific situation about which you have not sought the Lord's guidance? ○ yes ○ no
If so, why have you not sought Him?

_____

I meet so many believers who love the Lord and live holy lives, yet seem to be missing something in their Christian experience. I, too, have lived through years of mediocre Christianity where I haven't experienced His power, felt His presence, or heard His voice. As I searched Scripture and the Holy Spirit searched me, it became clear that I wasn't exercising an active faith that really believed God would do for me those things He did for believers in Bible times. If we want to hear God speak, we have to exercise active faith, believing He will work in our lives.

Draw a line from the Scripture to God's corresponding activity.

Genesis 1:3	to accomplish
Isaiah 55:11	to calm
Mark 4:39	to resurrect
Luke 8:53-54	to create
Luke 13:12	to heal

Which of these works of God do you need to see most evidenced in your life right now? In what way?

_____

_____

Faith is the channel of living trust that allows us to experience God in our everyday lives. He is looking for someone who believes He is who He says He is and He can do what He says He can do! Go to God expecting to hear His voice, and don't hesitate to move forward in obedience. When you obey, you move from your agenda to His, and God's plan is always greater.

HIS WORD IS ENOUGH

John 4:46-54 tells the story of a royal official of Capernaum whose son was sick to the point of death. He had so much faith in the power of God's Word that he walked about 20 miles from Capernaum to Cana just to see Jesus. When he met with Jesus there, he requested that Jesus come to heal his son. Jesus responded by saying, "Go, your son lives." The official "believed the word that Jesus spoke to him and started off" (v. 50).

How did the official's action demonstrate His faith in Jesus' word?

_____

The official had no evidence that Jesus' words had made any change in the life of his son since he was 20 miles away. His faith alone gave him the assurance to take the journey home. Can you imagine how agonizing that trip would have been for someone who didn't trust what Jesus said? This man believed the word of Jesus enough to confidently walk back home. When his servants came running to meet him, they told him his son had been healed; and when they compared the time of Jesus' words with the time the son's health returned, the two were the same.

If the official had not believed Jesus' word, instead of walking confidently toward home, how might his response have differed?

_____

God's Word is enough! Having faith like the royal official will enable us to walk in confidence even when all we have to hold to is His Word. If God has spoken to you clearly about something, start moving toward it so you don't miss the glorious moment when your faith will become sight.

What has the Holy Spirit taught you as you studied today?

_____

_____

_____

What is God asking you to do as a result of today's study?

_____

_____

Write a prayer responding to God's commands to you.

_____

_____

_____

THIS WEEK AT A GLANCE

Write the key principles from this week's study:

Day 1: _____

_____

Day 2: _____

_____

Day 3: _____

_____

Day 4: _____

_____

Day 5: _____

_____

Look back at your notes from the end of each day of study. List three things the Holy Spirit has encouraged you to do as a result of this week's study.

1. _____

2. _____

3. _____

What immediate steps will you take to respond in obedience?

_____

_____

_____

_____

THE HOLY SPIRIT

When you heard the word of truth, the gospel of your salvation—in Him when you believed—
were sealed with the promised Holy Spirit. He is the down payment of our inheritance,
for the redemption of the possession, to the praise of His glory.
Ephesians 1:13-14, HCSB

The Holy Spirit is the _____ _____ God guides His believers today.

The Holy Spirit, all of the Holy Spirit, _____ every believer.

Every person, whether believer or nonbeliever, is made up of _____,
_____, and _____.

When you become a believer, the _____ takes up residence in you.

Every person, whether believer or nonbeliever, has a conscience that is part of the _____.

The conscience is _____ the voice of God.

When you think the Holy Spirit is leading you, look for

1. the witness of the _____ _____.

2. the illumination of the _____.

3. the confirmation of God's hand in _____.

The Five Ms of Correctly Hearing God

1. Look for the _____ of the _____.

2. Live in the _____ of _____.

3. Search out the _____ of _____.

4. Submit to the _____ of _____.

5. Expect the _____ of _____.

The Holy Spirit

Day 1 — THE MIRACLE OF THE HOLY SPIRIT

HE SPEAKS
*The LORD our
God has shown us
His glory and His
greatness, and we
have heard His
voice ... we have
seen today that God
speaks with man.
Deuteronomy 5:24*

*FAR BE IT FROM ME TO DENY that spectacular experiences
occur or that they are, sometimes at least, given by God. But ... the
still small voice—or the interior or inner voice, as it is also called—is
the preferred and most valuable form of individualized communication
for God's purposes.[1] —Dallas Willard*

Old and New Testament Scriptures provide an account of the miraculous ways
God spoke to His children. I often wish that a visible sign, like the cloud that led
the children of Israel by day or the pillar of fire that led them by night, would
supernaturally appear in my life when I need to make a decision. It seems the
clearest way to know God's voice.

When God chose to speak in the Bible, those who heard didn't doubt
whether God had spoken or what He was asking them to do. He made His Word
clear. The primary method God uses to speak has changed, but His goal has not.
He wants His children to hear, recognize, and obey His voice.

The primary method God uses to speak has changed, but His

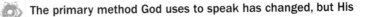

_____ has not.

I have not normally heard God in the miraculous ways God chose to speak to Old Testament believers. My experience, however, doesn't mean God no longer speaks in miraculous ways. Unless the Scripture clearly teaches otherwise, we must leave room for God to be God. He alone can choose how He speaks to us. When God does choose to speak in miraculous ways today, they will serve not as the *foundation* for us to hear from God but as *confirmation* of the Holy Spirit's leading and the message of Scripture.

How does Hebrews 1:1-4 tell us God spoke to the apostolic age?

_____

How do John 16:13 and Romans 8:14b suggest God speaks to His people from the beginning of the books of Acts to the present time?

_____

Answer the following statements as true (T) or false (F).
_____ 1. God can speak using any method He chooses.
_____ 2. Today God usually speaks through visible signs.
_____ 3. God chooses to speak to me predominantly through His Spirit and His Word.
_____ 4. If God uses some sensational means to speak, I should rely on this over what the Spirit has revealed in Scripture.
_____ 5. If God uses sensational means to speak to me, it will only confirm what His Word and His Spirit say.

Statements 1, 3, and 5 are true. God has primarily chosen to speak through His Word and His Spirit today. Any sensational means the Lord uses to speak will confirm what He's already saying.

When God does choose to speak in miraculous ways today, they will serve not as the foundation for us to hear from God but as confirmation of the Holy Spirit's leading and the message of Scripture.

Sensational means appealing to the five senses

❧ HE SPEAKS TO ME ❧

For several weeks I sensed the Lord wanted to take me in a new direction spiritually and personally. We needed to make some decisions regarding our ministry that were going to stretch my faith and challenge me. It would be far more comfortable for me to stay where I was and cling to what God had already done in the past. But in my prayer time and Bible study, I sensed the Holy Spirit pulling me forward.

I attended a new Bible study during this time. I didn't know anyone in the group and no one knew me. At the end of the message, the teacher looked my direction and said, "I feel prompted to share Isaiah 43:18-19 with you. It says, 'Forget about what's happened. Don't keep going over old history. Be alert, be present. I'm about to do something brand new. It's bursting out, don't you see it?'"

He continued, "The Lord wants to do something new in your life. What He has accomplished in your life has been extraordinary, but He doesn't want you to cling to it anymore. He has something new for you, your family, and your ministry." This message confirmed what the Holy Spirit had already been telling me.

Have you ever heard from the Lord in a sensational way?

O yes O no   If yes, how did this confirm what God was saying

to you? _____

❧ THANK GOD FOR THE HOLY SPIRIT ❧

John 16:7
I tell you the
truth, it is to your
advantage that I
go away; for if
I do not go away,
the Helper will not
come to you; but
if I go, I will send
Him to you.

In the Old Testament, the Holy Spirit was only given to specific people to achieve specific tasks. Old Testament believers had to count on external means to hear God because they didn't have continuous access to the Holy Spirit.

The disciples didn't see losing Jesus as an advantage, but He said they would be better off after He was gone (see John 16:7 in margin). The Holy Spirit would be a constant source of companionship and guidance in the lives of those who believe. He would reveal the mind of God to each person continuously and individually (see 1 Cor. 2:10).

While we often wish we had what the Old Testament believers had, they probably wanted what we have: direct, personal access to God.

Describe the differences between God's guidance to Old Testament believers and how God chooses to lead you.

_____

Why is this to your advantage?

_____

We shouldn't say God can't speak in miraculous ways today, but we shouldn't rely on these means of hearing God. He has not promised to lead us in a way that appeals to our senses; rather, He has promised to lead us in a way that appeals to our spirits—the leading of the Holy Spirit within us (see Rom. 8:14).

What has the Holy Spirit taught you as you studied today?

_____

_____

What is God asking you to do as a result of today's study?

_____

_____

_____

Write a prayer responding to God's commands to you.

_____

_____

_____

---

1. Dallas Willard, *Hearing God: Developing a Conversational Relationship with God* (Downers Grove, IL: InterVarsity Press, 1999), 89.

Day 2 THE CONSCIENCE AND THE HOLY SPIRIT

I KNOW THE LORD IS SPEAKING TO ME *when I stop listening to sounds from the world that feed my sense of pride and ambition. Instead, I fall quiet, tune in to God's great world around me, and actively listen. Sometimes nature speaks, telling me of God's majesty and glory. Sometimes God's Word speaks, reminding me of what God wants me to know. And sometimes the Spirit speaks, awakening my conscience, reminding me of failures, stirring my compassion and sense of justice, aligning me with God's will. I cannot control the voice of God or how it comes. I can only control my "ears"—my readiness to listen and quickness to respond. —Philip Yancey*

HE SPEAKS

The spirit of man is the lamp of the LORD.
Proverbs 20:27

❧ THE VOICE OF THE HOLY SPIRIT ❧

Our spirits are the core and essence of who we are. Likewise, every human has a deep inner voice called a conscience. This voice guides and directs our choices. It's that sense deep inside that you should or shouldn't do or say something. Even non-Christians can be moral people. Their conscience helps direct their choices.

> Share a time when you followed your conscience to make a life decision.

_____

The problem with following your conscience is that every person's conscience is formed and developed based on their personal environment and specific life circumstances. Each person's conscience has been shaped by the tradition and truth or lies to which it has been exposed.

Rebecca was reared in a home where all the women were divorced. In her family, divorcing for trivial reasons and remarrying was the norm. As a result, she learned to think this was normal and acceptable. She struggles with thoughts of divorce in her own marriage because of the tradition of her family.

Like Rebecca, our conscience can be shaped in a way that is not pleasing to the Lord. This can hinder our ability to clearly hear what the Holy Spirit is saying to us.

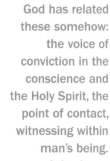

I believe that God has related these somehow: the voice of conviction in the conscience and the Holy Spirit, the point of contact, witnessing within man's being. It is always perilous to resist the conscience within.[1]
—A.W. Tozer

❧ THE AWAKENING OF THE CONSCIENCE ❧

When you become a Christian, your spirit becomes new. You don't become *changed*, you become *exchanged*. The Spirit of the Living God indwells your human spirit. He gives you new life (see 2 Cor. 5:17; Titus 3:5).

✿ **When I became a Christian, I didn't become _____,**

I became _____.

Now that you have been exchanged as a believer, your spirit is under the control of the Holy Spirit. God begins to change your mind, will, and emotions to reflect His thoughts and feelings. As you surrender your life and obey His written Word, He begins to reprogram your conscience. Your Spirit-led conscience starts to discern between sin and righteousness and instructs you accordingly (see John 16:8).

On the left side of the chart below, write an action or thought pattern you once practiced. On the right side, detail how your actions and attitudes have changed since the Holy Spirit took up residence in your life. I've given you one of my examples.

Before Salvation	**After Salvation**
Overeating was OK	Convicted about the sin of gluttony

_____ _____

_____ _____

_____ _____

_____ _____

_____ _____

_____ _____

❧ KNOWING IF IT IS REALLY GOD ❧

We must develop spiritual ears to hear the Spirit's leading. There are guidelines we can follow to help us be sure we are hearing our Spirit-led conscience accurately. I call them the five Ms of correctly hearing God.

1. *Look for the message of the Spirit.* Listen to the Holy Spirit. Don't just casually ask God for guidance. Consciously turn your attention inward to see if what you are sensing carries the weight of God or if it is the unsure, unsteady voice of your own conscience.

2. *Live in the mode of prayer.* Submit what you hear back to God in prayer. Throughout your day when the issue comes into your mind, don't spend time worrying; spend time handing the issue over to God.

3. *Search out the model of Scripture.* Carefully consider the Scriptures. Does what you think you're hearing in any way contradict the character of God or the Word of God?

4. *Submit to the ministry of Eli.* Seek the counsel of a wise, more mature believer who can discern God's leading in his or her own life.

5. *Expect the mercy of confirmation.* Ask the Lord for confirmation.

God desires for you to know His will. He's not hiding it from you. When I ask the Lord to confirm what He is saying to me through the Holy Spirit so I can be sure He is indeed speaking, He allows the Holy Spirit to speak to me and verify His message through His written Word, circumstances, or even another person.

The Five Ms of Correctly Hearing God

1. Look for the message of the Spirit.
2. Live in the mode of prayer.
3. Search out the model of Scripture.
4. Submit to the ministry of Eli.
5. Expect the mercy of confirmation.

❦ CONSCIENCE CONFIRMATION ❦

A few days ago I felt God showing me that He wanted to cut some things from my life so I could focus more on my relationship with Him. After seeking Him in prayer, I asked Him for confirmation. My Bible study that day was on Deuteronomy 30:6: "The LORD your God will circumcise your heart and the heart of your descendants, to love the LORD your God with all your heart and with all your soul, so that you may live." When I opened a book later that day, the section I was reading was entitled "A Circumcised Heart." At Bible study that week, my leader told me he sensed I was about to experience a shaking in my life for the purpose of getting rid of that which kept me from being fully His. God emphatically confirmed His word.

> Think of a time you sensed the Spirit leading you. Write a plan in the margin detailing what you will do to clarify God's leading. Use the five Ms to construct your plan.

What has the Holy Spirit taught you as you studied today?

_____

_____

What is God asking you to do as a result of today's study?

_____

_____

_____

Write a prayer responding to God's commands to you.

_____

_____

_____

---

1. A.W. Tozer, quoted in *Hearing God* (Grand Rapids: Baker Books, 1988), 20.

Day 3 THE GUIDANCE OF THE HOLY SPIRIT

WHAT HINDERS ME FROM HEARING *is that I am taken up with other things. It is not that I will not hear God, but I am not devoted in the right place. I am devoted to things, to service, to convictions, and God may say what He likes, but I do not hear Him. The child attitude is always, "Speak, Lord, for Thy servant heareth."*[1]
—*Oswald Chambers*

HE SPEAKS
All who are led by the Spirit of God are children of God.
Romans 8:14, NLT

I take many plane rides, but one stands out in my memory. I was enjoying the ride and reading a book as the plane sailed through the air. Suddenly we were shaken from our seats as the aircraft seemed to fall for a few moments before regaining composure. Passengers screamed, overhead compartments opened, and bags flew across the aisles.

After a few moments the pilot explained what had happened. The control tower had radioed to tell him we were on a collision course with another airplane. If we didn't take immediate evasive action, people would be hearing about a major disaster on the evening news. The pilot apologized but told us it was his only option to keep us safe. The control tower's ability to see the whole picture and the pilot's willingness to trust its guidance saved our lives.

The Holy Spirit is God's control tower. He sees the end from the beginning and seeks to guide us though this life.

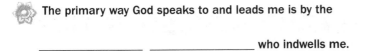

The primary way God speaks to and leads me is by the

_____ _____ **who indwells me.**

IGNORING THE CONTROL TOWER

The Holy Spirit will never tell us to do anything that isn't in God's will. He speaks exactly what He hears from the Father. He begins to influence our minds, will, emotions, and bodies to desire what is pleasing to God and will bring Him glory. Our responsibility is to cooperate by obeying His promptings and bathing ourselves in the Word and in prayer.

In what ways are you cooperating with the Holy Spirit?

_____

In what ways are you resisting?

_____

CONCENTRATING ON THE CONSCIENCE

The Holy Spirit is transforming your conscience into Christlikeness. He guides your conscience to convict you and speak to you concerning God's plan for you.

The more you develop your relationship with the Lord, the more you can rely on your conscience for guidance, not because it is infallible but because God is. The more you come to recognize God's voice and practice your ability to discern God's leading, the easier it will be for you to know when God is talking. We can always submit what we think we are hearing from God to the five Ms.

Review the five Ms of correctly hearing God on page 33 and write them in the margin.

Since the Holy Spirit seeks to fill you and control your conscience in an effort to direct your decisions, He will confirm what He is saying in the small details as well as the major decisions you have to make. As we seek to be more spirit-conscious, we should focus on the Spirit as our source of guidance. This means we foster an environment where the Holy Spirit can flourish, fill, and clearly speak to us.

FOCUSING ON THE CONTROL TOWER

1 Thessalonians 5:23

May your spirit and soul and body be preserved complete, without blame at the coming of our Lord Jesus Christ.

We have to retrain ourselves to let our Spirit-led conscience be our guide and dominate our decision making. We are naturally more body-conscious, mind-conscious, and emotion-conscious than spirit-conscious.

Read 1 Thessalonians 5:23 in the margin. Notice the order of the underlined words. What might Paul be trying to emphasize?

_____

Most of us spend more time emphasizing our bodies and souls than our spirits. We want to do what feels good, appeases our emotions, seems rational to our mind, and suits our will—with little thought to what the "control tower" is saying in us. The Holy Spirit sees the whole picture and may want to reveal something beyond what our physical senses can comprehend.

1 Timothy 4:7-8, NLT
Spend your time and energy in training yourself for spiritual fitness. Physical exercise has some value, but spiritual exercise is much more important, for it promises a reward in both this life and the next.

How do we begin focusing on the control tower within? We begin our day surrendering ourselves to Him and asking Him to heighten our spiritual senses to see and hear Him throughout the day. Then, as we do the mundane tasks that consume our lives, we purposefully turn our awareness inward and say, "God, what do you think?"

As we put our attention on the Spirit, something miraculous takes place. Not only do we more clearly distinguish God's word to us, but the desires of our bodies and souls begin to fall in line with God's.

The Holy Spirit has begun the work of sanctifying you so that your desires more closely mirror His. You can cooperate with Him through obedience and spending intimate time with Him.

What has the Holy Spirit taught you as you studied today?

_____

_____

Romans 8:5, NLT
Those who are controlled by the Holy Spirit think about things that please the Spirit.

What is God asking you to do as a result of today's study?

_____

_____

_____

Write a prayer responding to God's commands to you.

_____

_____

_____

_____

---

1. Oswald Chambers, *My Utmost for His Highest* (Westwood, NJ: Barbour Books, 1988), 32.

Day 4   TRANSFORMED BY THE HOLY SPIRIT

I BELIEVE IN THE TRUTH *found in Romans 12:1-2. If I have presented my body to Him as a living sacrifice, and I have, and I'm being transformed by the renewing of my mind then I'm able to prove—to put to the text—what His will is. He will show me that which is good, acceptable, and perfect for me. —Kay Arthur*

You include three parts. Your spirit allows contact with the spiritual realm. Your soul allows you access to your emotions and mind. You body relates with the physical realm through the five senses. As you yield to and obey the Holy Spirit's leading in your life, He conforms your soul to the image of Christ and uses your body as the instrument to carry out His purposes.

 As I yield to and obey the Holy Spirit's leading in my life, He

conforms my soul to the _____ of Christ and uses

my body as the instrument to carry out His _____.

❧ DEALING WITH OUR BODIES ❧

Have you ever sat in front of a piece of chocolate cake or some other indulgence and felt you couldn't help but take a bite? My stomach can be completely full, but my mouth is determined to taste the chocolate. I know that when I finish the cake I will regret eating it, but I do it anyway.

We often have the same struggle in the spiritual realm. The indwelling Holy Spirit tells us what is best for us, but our flesh says the opposite. Paul was one of the most godly men in history, but he had this same struggle. He writes one of the clearest descriptions of the battle between the flesh and the spirit in Romans 7.

Read Romans 7:14-19 in the margin on page 39. How does this battle between the flesh and spirit most often impact you?

- ○ pride   ○ anger   ○ lust
- ○ gluttony   ○ envy   ○ other _____

In Romans 12:1, Paul tells us how to experience victory with our bodies as we seek to follow the leading of our Spirit. He says, "Present your bodies a living and holy sacrifice." Paul didn't say to experience victory in this area you have to fight really hard. He just said to present, yield, or surrender your body. Through Jesus you have already been given victory as a gift (see 1 Cor. 15:57). You experience it by presenting your body to God as an instrument for Him to use.

The Holy Spirit is always busy making us like Jesus, but we must cooperate in this effort. We must reformat our thinking to understand that every part of our body has been given to us not for our own gratification but as a "tool to do what is right for the glory of God" (Rom. 6:13, NLT). Give your hands to Him for His work, your feet to walk His path, and your ears to hear Him speak.

> On the following list, circle the part of your body you most struggle to present to God as a living sacrifice.
> mind—what I think about   mouth—what I say
> eyes—what I see   ears—what I listen to
> hands—what I do   feet—where I go
> other _____
>
> Why do you think you find it difficult to yield this area to God?
>
> _____

An African missionary once told a group of people that each morning, before he got up, he would take time to present himself to God. He would stretch out across his bed and picture the bed as an altar on which he was the sacrifice. He started each day by saying, "Lord, this day I present myself as a tool for You. Today I am Your living sacrifice."

DEALING WITH OUR SOULS

My husband was satisfied with his corporate job when out of nowhere God told him to leave so we could work together in ministry. Jerry thought it was absurd. He had worked a normal 8–5 job with good pay and benefits most of his life and was quickly climbing the ladder of success at his company. Doing something unconventional like self-employed ministry seemed illogical. Yet the Holy Spirit would not let him rest. It became clear through the Spirit's leading, prayer, wise counsel, and confirmation through the Word and other circumstances that God was leading him in that direction despite the way he felt.

Often the Spirit's leading will contradict our logic and feelings; but when we submit, we will experience a deep-rooted peace about our decision.

Romans 7:14-19
I am of flesh, sold into bondage to sin. For what I am doing, I do not understand; for I am not practicing what I would like to do, but I am doing the very thing I hate. But if I do the very thing I do not want to do, I agree with the Law, confessing that the Law is good. So now, no longer am I the one doing it, but sin which dwells in me. For I know that nothing good dwells in me, that is, in my flesh; for the willing is present in me, but the doing of the good is not. For the good that I want, I do not do, but I practice the very evil that I do not want.

In addition to being involved in spiritual matters, the soul is involved in the things of this world. But when we turn our backs on Him, exposing our souls to the world, He will not so easily answer our call. When we are willing to accept God's help and guard our souls according to His desires, we may commune with Him whenever we like.[1]
—Brother Lawrence

When we become Christians, the Holy Spirit begins to sanctify us and change our personalities to suit His design. We assist in the process of conforming to His image through obedience to His Word. As the Spirit conforms us to the image of Christ, the gap between His desires and ours narrows. God put His thought in Jerry's mind and, over time, Jerry's feelings radically changed. He began to feel it was foolish to stay at his old job when God was giving him an opportunity to work full time for the kingdom of God.

The book of James was written to believers whose spirits had already been made new through salvation. But the author gave the believers startling instructions in James 1:21. Look up this passage in your Bible and fill in the blanks.

"Putting aside all _____ and all that remains of

_____, in humility receive the _____

implanted, which is able to _____" (NASB).

James tells us our souls still need to be saved. The soul still contains "filthiness and all that remains of wickedness." Our spirits were reborn when we received Christ, but our souls need to be renewed. The Spirit is at work to make this happen, but we must cooperate.

If we want to hear God's voice clearly, we need to immerse ourselves in the Word of God. As we hear Him speak through His Word, He works in us to radically change us (see 2 Thess. 2:13 in margin). When you take in God's Word, massive renovation takes place on the inside. Your very soul is being renewed. Cooperate with what the Holy Spirit is doing in your life.

What has the Holy Spirit taught you as you studied today?

_____

_____

2 Thessalonians 2:13
God has chosen you from the beginning for salvation through sanctification by the Spirit and faith in the truth.

What is God asking you to do as a result of today's study?

_____

_____

_____

_____

Write a prayer responding to God's commands to you.

_____

_____

_____

1. Brother Lawrence, *The Practice of the Presence of God* (Springdale, PA: Whitaker House, 1982), 9.

Day 5 LED BY THE HOLY SPIRIT

I KNOW THE LORD IS SPEAKING *to me when He impresses something on my Spirit internally and confirms it through a person or circumstance externally.* —Tony Evans

HE SPEAKS
This is the new covenant I will make with the people … I will put my laws in their minds so they will understand them, and I will write them on their hearts so they will obey them.
Hebrews 8:10, NLT

When I was pregnant with my first son, I began a love affair with chocolate. I never had a taste for it until my eighth month. Something happened that changed my taste buds; I had never desired chocolate. Now I can't get enough!

When the new life of the Holy Spirit takes up residence in you, He begins to change your taste buds. Under the new covenant described in Hebrews 8:10, the Holy Spirit will allow you to hear His voice and cause you to understand and desire God's will for you. This is the essence of hearing God's voice.

FREEDOM TO HEAR GOD

We look around every corner to discover God's will. We often carry a load of responsibility because we wonder if our decisions are in God's will. Desiring and doing His will is not our responsibility to discover; it's His responsibility to reveal.

 Desiring and doing His will is not my responsibility to

_____; **it's His responsibility to** _____.

Philippians 2:13
*It is God who
is at work in you,
both to will and
to work for His
good pleasure.*

Read Philippians 2:13 in the margin. Paul reiterated the point of this verse in Philippians 3:15 (margin). In Philippians 3:15, circle the portion that reveals your responsibility, and underline the portion that indicates God's responsibility.

Paul encouraged them to have the attitude of perseverance in knowing and doing God's will and assured them that if at any time they stepped away from what God desired, the Lord would let them know. God is doing everything to reveal His will and cause us to go after it! Through the Holy Spirit, "He writes His laws on our hearts and on our minds, and we love them, and are drawn, by our affections and judgment, not driven, to our obedience."[1]

Philippians 3:15
*Let us therefore,
as many as are
[mature], have this
attitude; and if in
anything you have
a different attitude,
God will reveal
that also to you.*

No longer do I frantically search for God's will; I frantically search for God. I trust that it is His responsibility to show me what He wants me to do and how to do it by speaking through the Holy Spirit and the Word of God. As I seek Him, stay in His Word, and continue to keep an intimate relationship with Him by confessing my sin, He transforms my mind and emotions to align with His plans.

What is the difference between seeking God's will and seeking Him?

_____

**No longer do
I frantically
search for
God's will;
I frantically
search for
God.**

❧ PUT MY LAWS IN THEIR MINDS ❧

I will never forget reading Psalm 46:10 in February 1997. I had read this verse many times before, but this time it was as if for the first time. I was tired emotionally and physically. As the familiar words of this verse washed over me, I saw it with new eyes and heard the Holy Spirit speak, "Cease striving and know that I am God." A feeling of peace and serenity washed over me as the Lord removed my burden. I knew the Holy Spirit had caused me to see something with my spiritual eyes that day instead of my physical eyes. All of a sudden I understood the verse. It became relevant for me. He was writing His law on my mind.

Read 2 Corinthians 3:14-17 in your Bible and answer the following:

When the law of Moses was read under the old covenant, what effect did it have on the hearer (v. 15)?

_____

What is the only thing that can lift the veil of understanding for an individual (v. 16)?

_____

The Word of God given without the clarity of the Holy Spirit will not penetrate the hearer's understanding. Only by His Spirit can the veil be lifted from our eyes to understand God's Word so that we desire to put it into practice. As a Christian, you have been given the right and privilege not only to hear God's voice, but to understand it so that it can penetrate your heart. As you look into the Bible, He will enable you to not only read what is written but hear how it applies to your life and specific situations. Only the Spirit in you can make this happen.

> What do you feel the Lord leading you to do right now that goes against the way you feel?

_____

> What is something you desire right now but are not sure it is God's desire for you?

_____

The Holy Spirit has taken up residence in you and me. He is changing our tastes to suit what pleases Him. When you delight yourself in Him, you can relax in knowing that He will speak clearly to you, order your steps, and cause you to desire what brings Him pleasure.

What has the Holy Spirit taught you as you studied today?

_____

_____

What is God asking you to do as a result of today's study?

_____

_____

Write a prayer of commitment to God regarding what He is asking you to do.

_____

_____

He will take possession of our will and work it for us. ... His suggestions will come to us ... as desires springing up within. They will originate in our will; we shall feel as though we wanted to do so and so, not as though we must. And this makes a service of perfect liberty; for it is always easy to do what we desire to do, let the accompanying circumstances be as difficult as they may.[2]
—Hannah Whitall Smith

1. Hannah Whitall Smith, *The Christian's Secret of a Happy Life* (New York City: Grosset and Dunlap, n.d.), 76.
2. Ibid.

∽ THIS WEEK AT A GLANCE ∽

Write the key principles from this week's study:

Day 1: _____

_____

Day 2: _____

_____

Day 3: _____

_____

Day 4: _____

_____

Day 5: _____

_____

Look back at your notes from the end of each day of study. List three things the Holy Spirit has encouraged you to do as a result of this week's study.

1. _____

2. _____

3. _____

What immediate steps will you take to respond in obedience?

_____

_____

_____

_____

THE VOICE OF THE HOLY SPIRIT

When the Spirit of truth comes, He will guide you into all the truth.
For He will not speak on His own, but He will speak whatever He hears.
He will also declare to you what is to come.
John 16:13, HCSB

When we go through life, we need a _____ we can trust.

The Holy Spirit asks us to _____ to Him, to _____ Him, and to _____ Him.

John 16:13—*When the Spirit of truth comes, He will* _____.

"To guide" means to lead while one is _____.

The Holy Spirit offers you _____ truth.

The Holy Spirit guides you with _____ truth.

The Holy Spirit guides you into an _____ truth.

_____ prevent you from hearing the voice of God.

Combat strongholds by _____ them with _____ weapons.

WEEK 3

The Voice of the Holy Spirit

Day 1   PERSISTENT

HE SPEAKS
*Once God has
spoken;
Twice I have
heard this:
That power
belongs to God.
Psalm 62:11*

THE LORD LEADS US THROUGH *His Word, through feelings
and through circumstances, and mostly through all three together. It
is such a wonderful experience when the Lord speaks through our
feelings and our thinking when we pray and listen to the Lord. The
prayer becomes then a conversation from both sides. We on our side
must ... expect that the Lord acts according to His promises and
leads us on His way.*[1] *—Corrie Ten Boom*

Last week we looked at the Holy Spirit and how He indwells us—the primary
way God leads us. This week, let's look more closely at the things that often
characterize the Holy Spirit's leadings and how He works to cause us to recognize His promptings.

From the Old Testament to the New, we see a God who persistently calls to
His children in an attempt to turn their ears and actions in His direction. Time
after time, He gave His children opportunity to recognize Him. Thankfully, He
continued to pursue them even when they didn't initially respond.

The Holy Spirit works in our hearts, in the hearts of others, and in the
events of our lives to point us in His direction. He uses all these things to cause
us to hear and heed His voice.

God _____ calls me in an attempt to turn my

_____ and _____ in His direction.

Read each Scripture passage in your Bible and answer the following questions.

1 Samuel 3:1-10—How many times did God call before Samuel

recognized His voice? _____

Who did God use to help Samuel recognize His voice?

_____

1 Samuel 3:19,21—Even though Samuel took a while to recognize and respond to God's voice, what happened?

_____

John 4:7-26—How many times did the Lord speak to the

Samaritan woman in this passage? _____

What words prove that she did not know she was speaking

to the Messiah? _____

What words did the Lord use to clearly identify Himself?

_____

The Lord used another person to help Samuel recognize God's leading. For the woman at the well, He identified Himself through His own spoken word. In both cases, it took several tries for the listeners to realize to Whom they were speaking. God is persistent!

MORE THAN FATE

One of my favorite movies is *Serendipity.* In the movie, a series of unexplainable events bring a man and a woman together despite unbelievable odds. Everywhere they turn they are brought face-to-face with their destiny—one another.

People use the word *serendipity* to infer that the stars have aligned and the circumstances of their lives have persistently pointed them in a direction. The unbelieving person would call it karma, fate, or coincidence. But the believer knows that behind serendipity stands the sovereign One who seeks to speak to us and lead us in His ways. What others see as signs, we see as God's continual confirmation of His will. When He speaks to you internally, and then causes other events to confirm what He is saying, you should be on the lookout for God's direction. When God speaks, He does so persistently.

I remember a time I felt inner conviction to apologize to someone. I tried to resist it, but I knew God was leading me to do it. That day one of my favorite talk shows was discussing the importance of saying "I'm sorry." That evening my personal Bible study time just happened to be about going to a brother or sister in Christ to ask forgiveness and restore peace. Mere coincidence? I think not!

> Have you ever had a similar experience when God used multiple things to confirm what He was trying to tell you? ○ yes ○ no

> If yes, what persistent naggings did you experiencing in your spirit?

> _____

> What other events reinforced what you sensed the Lord asking you

> to do? _____

> _____

Some of the most godly people I know learned to hear God by trial and error. Sometimes they got it right and sometimes they didn't, but God used each mistake to teach them a lesson about hearing His voice. He continued to pursue them and continues to pursue us. If you notice that a message seems to be confirmed persistently through Scripture, circumstances, and the leading of the Holy Spirit, pay close attention.

> Read Job 33:15-22 in the margin and underline each way God chose to speak.

God didn't call to these people once and then throw His hands up in the air. He kept at it. As we seek Him and acknowledge Him, He promises to continue to direct our paths (Prov. 3:5-6), and often does so by bombarding us with a thought that will not cease to permeate our thoughts and hearts. When you are walking with Him, seeking Him, and desiring to receive His direction, He will direct you with consistent persistence.

Job 33:15-22, NLT
He speaks in dreams, in visions of the night when deep sleep falls on people as they lie in bed. He whispers in their ear and terrifies them with his warning. He causes them to change their minds; he keeps them from pride. He keeps them from the grave, from crossing over the river of death. Or God disciplines people with sickness and pain, with ceaseless aching in their bones. They lose their appetite and do not care for even the most delicious food. They waste away to skin and bones. They are at death's door; the angels of death wait for them.

THAT PESKY NEIGHBOR

One day my neighbor knocked on the door. I wasn't in the mood for company and wasn't particularly dressed for it, so I stayed tucked away in my room and tried to ignore her. I figured that after a few unanswered knocks, she would go away. She didn't. She kept banging on the door without mercy. After several long minutes, I begrudgingly went to the door and opened it. She had come over to tell me she had seen smoke coming from the side of my house. I was so thankful for her relentless attempts to get my attention.

Revelation 3:20 was written to a group of people who already believed in the Messiah, the church in Laodicea. Christ tells these believers that He will keep knocking on the doors of their hearts so that sweet intimacy can take place. Despite their lukewarm relationship with Him, He still pursued them, continued knocking, and desired deeper levels of fellowship. Even though they were already believers, His pursuit of them didn't stop. He wanted more and was willing to keep on knocking until they opened the door and let Him in to "dine with him, and he with Me."

Revelation 3:20
I stand at the door and knock; if anyone hears My voice and opens the door, I will come in to him and will dine with him, and he with Me.

What has the Holy Spirit taught you as you studied today?

_____

_____

_____

What is God asking you to do as a result of today's study?

_____

_____

Write a prayer responding to God's commands to you.

_____

_____

_____

_____

1. Corrie Ten Boom, *Marching Orders for the End Battle* (Fort Washington, PA: Christian Literature Crusade, 1969), 75.

Day 2   PERSONAL

HE SPEAKS

To one who knows the right thing to do and does not do it, to him it is sin.

James 4:17

WHEN HE SPEAKS, IT'S IN *the language of our own personal lives, through a verse or passage of Scripture that just seems to leap up off the page with our name on it.*[1] —*Anne Graham Lotz*

Michelle is a godly women with an admirable intimacy with the Lord. I have long been impressed with her desire to follow the leading of the Holy Spirit. She listens to His voice of conviction and follows a code of conduct many would consider quite staunch and unnecessary. She avoids many movies, books, and television shows because of her personal convictions.

Several times our group has decided to do something that goes against Michelle's conviction. She always parts company with a smile. She doesn't try to impose her convictions on us or attempt to get us to change our plans to suit her. She just obediently responds to the leading of God in her life. She is committed to doing what the Lord has asked of her. Michelle knows that when the Holy Spirit leads, He does so personally and individually.

The Holy Spirit leads me _____ and _____.

Isaiah 45:3, NLT
I will give you treasures hidden in the darkness— secret riches. I will do this so you may know that I am the LORD, the God of Israel, the one who calls you by name.

❧ CALLED BY NAME ❧

When God spoke to a little boy, He called him by name, "Samuel, Samuel." When He wanted to capture the attention of a weary woman seeking the body of her crucified Lord at the tomb, He said, "Mary!" He astonished and changed a man traveling to Damascus when He called from a blinding light, "Saul, Saul." The directives He gave His followers were designed for them individually. God's clear usage of names when speaking to biblical characters gives us insight about how God speaks to His children today.

Scripture commands specific obedience of all believers on some matters. Some areas, however, change based on each individual and what the Lord wants to accomplish in her life. In these instances the Holy Spirit will "call us by name," giving us detailed directions tailored to our lives.

When God requires certain things of us, it's easy for us to assume He must be requiring it from everyone else as well. We might become legalistic and judgmental, placing other believers in bondage.

Have believers ever tried to hold you in bondage to their conviction? ○ yes ○ no If so, describe your experience below and be prepared to share it with your small group. Be careful not to slander or dishonor anyone in the process.

_____

_____

God has given us a combination of scriptural guidelines and freedom. Each believer must determine what God would have her do personally. The Holy Spirit knows your stage of spiritual development and will direct you accordingly. His job is to instruct you in the way you should go and give you specific details concerning the issues of your life.

For the woman called to be a full-time mom, the Holy Spirit may give a personal conviction about working outside the home. For the woman directed to lead Bible study, He may give a conviction about the time she chooses to spend in preparation. The Holy Spirit may guide the woman God leads to homeschool to avoid other educational options. All of these promptings by God are specifically designed to foster the needs of each woman and the needs of her loved ones.

Romans 14:16
Do not let what is for you a good thing be spoken of as evil.

SAME DESTINATION DIFFERENT DIRECTIONS

From where I live, the main road to downtown Dallas is Highway 35. I think it is the most efficient and obvious way for anyone to go downtown. But many people choose another route. Although I do tend to think my directions are the best, it doesn't mean they are the only way. These directions work for me, but another route may be best for someone else

As God leads us in our journey toward Him, we each follow different avenues. The Holy Spirit draws us individual maps to follow. Others may not choose our road, and they shouldn't if it's not a part of their map. We shouldn't challenge them regarding their chosen route unless it is an issue of scriptural principle. We should give others the freedom to enjoy the course they have prayerfully determined will be best for them.

Paul taught on this very issue in Romans 14. At the Christian church in Rome some of the believers were Jews and others were Gentiles. Their different cultural upbringings had caused each sector to have differing views on whether or not certain foods could be enjoyed. Paul used this issue as an illustration of how we should deal with our liberties in God and how we should treat others who think differently than we do.

1 Corinthians 8:12, NLT
You are sinning against Christ when you sin against other Christians by encouraging them to do something they believe is wrong.

Based on Romans 14:1-6, mark each statement true (T) or false (F).

_____ 1. My response to those who have different opinions from me should be acceptance (v. 1).

_____ 2. God has special favor on the one who chooses the action that appears to be most godly (v. 3).

_____ 3. I am not only accountable to my Master for my actions but also to other believers (v. 4).

_____ 4. As a Christian woman, I have a responsibility to judge others' actions (v. 4).

_____ 5. The only person who must be convinced about the actions I choose to take is me (v. 5).

_____ 6. The Holy Spirit could direct two people to do two different things, each equally glorifying to God (v. 6).

> I do not change my conviction based on what others are doing. Neither do I judge them based on what He has asked of me. These convictions are personal.

The Holy Spirit directs us according to His plan. His commands could lead two believers who equally love the Lord in opposite directions. As long as these actions both fall within the guidelines of Scripture and each person is following the Lord in obedience, both bring glory to God. Our responsibility is only to be sure we are following God's leading in our own lives. Numbers 1, 5, and 6 are true.

I do not change my conviction based on what others are doing. Neither do I judge them based on what He has asked of me. These convictions are personal.

Are you guilty of judging others based on your personal convictions? ○ yes ○ no ○ I'm not sure.
If so, in the margin list the initials of those you have judged.

Ask forgiveness for the judgment you have placed on them. As you offer each person to the Lord in prayer, place a line through their initials to symbolize their release from the bondage you have created. If your judgment has affected them, prayerfully consider asking for their forgiveness.

You are accountable to the Lord for what He personally requires of you. Going back to Paul's illustration about what foods the believer should eat, he said, "If people have doubts about whether they should eat something, they shouldn't eat it. They would be condemned for not acting in faith before God. If you do anything you believe is not right, you are sinning" (Rom. 14:23, NLT).

Is there an area of your life where the Lord is giving you personal instruction that you are not obeying? ○ yes ○ no

If so, what is keeping you from doing what He asks of you?

_____

Choose today not to rebel any longer. Yield to His personal word. It is tailored to produce spiritual fruit and guide you to the destination the Lord has for you.

What has the Holy Spirit taught you as you studied today?

_____

_____

What is God asking you to do as a result of today's study?

_____

_____

_____

Write a prayer responding to God's commands to you.

_____

_____

_____

---

1. Anne Graham Lotz, *My Heart's Cry* (Nashville: W Publishing Group, 2002), 11.

Day 3　PEACEFUL

HE SPEAKS

We pursue the things which make for peace and the building up of one another.
Romans 14:19

In college I was part of a Christian sorority that provided an alternative for Christian women who didn't want to be involved with the secular sororities. I enjoyed my time with this group but also chose to join another sorority on campus. Many girls genuinely believed that joining the secular sorority displeased God. I believed the Lord gave me the freedom to join.

My decision hurt many feelings and raised many questions. The worst part was that some fledgling believers struggled to make sense of what I had done. After all these years I look back and see that my freedom harmed other Christians and displeased God.

The Lord desires unity and mutual edification within the body of Christ. Scripture urges us to always keep ourselves "united in the Holy Spirit, and bind [ourselves] together with peace" (Eph. 4:3, NLT). Throughout the Bible, God's voice and His Word led His people to peaceable relationships with others.

God's _____ and His _____ lead me

to _____ relationships with others.

James 3:17, NLT
The wisdom that comes from heaven is first of all pure. It is also peace loving, gentle at all times, and willing to yield to others. It is full of mercy and good deeds. It shows no partiality and is always sincere.

Read James 3:17 in the margin. James describes how we can discern wisdom from God. Underline the words that emphasize the principle of today's lesson.

✦ FREEDOM TO FIND PEACE ✦

God will give you freedom to do things He may not give others freedom to do and vice versa. We must be careful, however, not to allow our freedom to harm other believers. Considering how our actions will affect others is a clear way the Holy Spirit allows us to determine what He is asking us to do at a particular time.

Yesterday we looked at Paul's illustration in Romans 14 concerning eating different types of food. Believers with Gentile backgrounds freely ate all things. Others with a Jewish background observed the ceremonial laws concerning food. They felt convicted about eating food that had been offered to idols. Paul encouraged each to remain true to his own conviction. He told those who felt God was allowing them to eat all foods to enjoy their freedom, but Paul also offered a warning.

Read Romans 14:19-20 in your Bible, focusing on verse 20.
What is the main principle Paul tried to address in this verse?

_____

Romans 14:15, NLT
If another Christian is distressed by what you eat, you are not acting in love if you eat it. Don't let your eating ruin someone for whom Christ died.

The work of God is more important than a trivial issue like what to eat. This more-important work is pursuing peace and building one another up. Paul made this clear when he said, "It is good not to eat meat or to drink wine, or to do anything by which your brother stumbles" (Rom. 14:21). Before we move forward in our freedoms, we need to be aware of how they will affect others.

When the Holy Spirit opens our eyes to see a fellow believer who will be hurt by what we are about to do, this is His way of saying, "Not now!" It doesn't mean we have lost that freedom, but rather that we are not to enjoy it right now. Keeping a fellow believer from stumbling trumps our personal freedoms.

A STUMBLING BLOCK

My sister Chrystal trips and falls more than anyone I know. We have had many laughs as a family about how clumsy she is. Whenever she is walking up or down stairs, my mother and I hold our breath in fear. We do everything in our power to clear the path for her and prevent a catastrophe.

As believers our goal should be to clear the path in front of those who are prone to stumble. We want to protect them from a weakened conscience or weakened commitment to the Lord. If we aren't careful, however, the Enemy can make the pressure of keeping our fellow believers safe an area of bondage for us. We can lose the ability to enjoy any freedoms because we constantly worry about how it will affect others.

As you exercise care about enjoying your freedoms, do not impede the spiritual progress of people who are moving forward and growing spiritually. These are people who have shown they are on a journey with God and are growing up and moving forward. We should show them our deepest regard to support their growth, not hinder it.

Can you think of people who fit this description in your life?
○ yes ○ no

If so, what is the Lord asking you to do in regard to them?

_____

_____

Describe the person Paul had in mind when he encouraged us to be careful about how we enjoy our liberties.

_____

_____

Being aware of how our actions will affect other believers is one way the Holy Spirit speaks to us. Have you ever considered this as an element of God's personal communication to you?

Choose three of the following verses. Read each from your Bible and record below how they speak to you regarding a current relationship in your life.

Psalm 34:14   Matthew 5:9   Mark 16:15
Romans 12:10   1 Corinthians 10:33   Colossians 3:15

1. _____

2. _____

3. _____

THE BOTTOM LINE

> You can always tell when a church or a family follows false wisdom: you will find jealousy, division, and confusion.[1]
> —W.W. Wiersbe

God loves unity and always encourages us to pursue peace. When determining whether or not you are hearing God's voice, ask yourself:

- Is the message I am hearing going to impede another believer's spiritual growth?
- Is the message I am hearing going to cause unnecessary conflict between myself and another believer?

If the answer to either of these questions is yes, ask the Lord for clarity before moving forward.

Pure, peaceable relationships are important to God. He will not lead us to hinder peace and unity in the body of Christ. This doesn't mean everyone will agree with what you are doing, but it does mean your decision will not cause another believer to stumble. God's word to you will not cause another believer to sin.

Take time to thank the Lord for the freedoms He has given you to enjoy, but also ask Him to make you sensitive to other believers.

What has the Holy Spirit taught you as you studied today?

_____

_____

_____

What is God asking you to do as a result of today's study?

_____

_____

Write a prayer responding to God's commands to you.

_____

_____

_____

_____

1. W. W. Wiersbe, *Wiersbe's Expository Outlines on the New Testament* (Wheaton, IL: Victor Books, 1997), 728.

Day 4 VERIFIABLE

WHEN YOU READ YOUR BIBLE, *receive and savor it ... like a love letter from God to you. Remember, you're reading in order to meet Someone. Ponder what you have read, and apply it to your present circumstances. Let it go down into the core of your being. And as you read, expect Him to commune with you.*[1]
—Bruce Wilkinson

HE SPEAKS
The word of God is living and active and sharper than any two-edged sword, and piercing as far as the division of soul and spirit, of both joints and marrow, and able to judge the thoughts and intentions of the heart.
Hebrews 4:12

I love to give gifts. What compares with seeing people's faces light up when they open a package specifically chosen for them?

Recently, I thought of bringing a small gift for a group of friends. I thought it would be a great idea and a way to bring joy to these gifted women. One day during my personal Bible study, however, I came across this verse: "When you give to someone, don't tell your left hand what your right hand is doing. Give your gifts in secret, and your Father, who knows all secrets, will reward you" (Matt. 6:3-4, NLT).

On that day, the familiar passage jumped off the page and seemed to be high-lighted just for me. As I thought about my gift idea in light of this verse, I began to question my motives. Was I doing it just because I wanted to do something nice and be a blessing, or did I desire to impress them and draw attention to myself?

I quickly realized that my flesh wanted glory and attention. This was the reason for my desire to give a gift on this occasion. Now when I feel led to give, I check to see if I am willing to do it in secret without reservation. This lets me know if I want God to get the glory or if I want it for myself.

How do you feel when you see another woman who obviously seeks attention for herself?

○ impressed   ○ repulsed   ○ pleased
○ angered   ○ other _____

What might the Holy Spirit save us from when He prompts us not to seek attention for ourselves?

_____

As the Lord has been teaching me to hear His voice, I am learning that the primary channel through which the Lord will reveal His word to me is the Bible. Scripture provides the boundaries into which all of God's fresh words will fall, even those words concerning our everyday lives.

 Scripture provides the _____ into which all of God's

fresh _____ will fall, even those words concerning

my _____ _____.

> **Anything God's Spirit reveals to you will *always* match up with what is in the Bible.**

Anything God's Spirit reveals to you will *always* match up with what is in the Bible, because all Scripture was given by the Holy Spirit (see 2 Tim. 3:16). He will never contradict Himself—no exceptions.

A friend of mine once had a young man ask for her hand in marriage, but he wasn't a Christian. She was very attracted to him. When he asked her to marry him, she had a strong desire to do so. But she knew this desire was not coming from the Holy Spirit, since He will never contradict Scripture, which says, "Do not be bound together with unbelievers" (2 Cor. 6:14).

Describe a time you felt the desire to do something that contradicted Scripture.

_____

_____

If you followed your feelings or intellect instead of Scripture, what happened as a result?

_____

If you followed Scripture, from what may God have saved you?

_____

Proverbs 14:12
There is a way which seems right to a [woman], But its end is the way of death.

HEARING GOD THROUGH HIS WORD

We can clearly hear from God on issues of principle such as the one my friend faced. Sadly, however, many stop looking to the Scripture when they can't find an answer to a specific problem. We need to change our thinking about the Bible. It is not just an old book with a lot of theology for us to digest; it is the living Word of God. When we read it, the Holy Spirit applies it to our particular situation regardless of how specific and personal it is.

I once asked Henry Blackaby to describe to me how he recognizes God's voice in his own life. He said, "[Recognizing God's voice] is really very simple. I always read the Word of God. The Holy Spirit uses the Word of God to bring me the mind and heart of God. When the Holy Spirit speaks through the Word of God I always know that I have the will of God and proceed."

As we seek to hear the Holy Spirit speak through Scripture, we are tuning our spiritual ears to catch the moment when a passage seems to capture our attention in an almost shocking way, a way through which our thoughts are drawn to how the passage applies to a specific situation in our lives. The Holy Spirit orchestrates these events. He speaks!

If I need God's direction regarding a particular situation, I ask the Lord for confirmation through His Word before moving forward. When the situation is particularly taxing and I am not sure what to do, I go into my time of Bible reading with prayer that clearly explains my need to the Lord. I request the Holy Spirit punctuate my time in His Word with clear direction, and I believe He will miraculously honor this request for all His children in His own timing.

We need to change our thinking about the Bible. It is not just an old book with a lot of theology for us to digest; it is the living Word of God.

The more Scripture you have hidden in your heart, the more opportunity He will have to bring it to your mind and direct you.

SATURATED IN THE WORD

The more Scripture you have hidden in your heart, the more opportunity He will have to bring it to your mind and direct you. Our goal should be to saturate ourselves in His Word.

How much time do you spend doing the following things?
Rank them 1 to 8, with 1 being the thing you spend the most time doing and 8 being what you spend the least time doing.

_____ reading God's Word _____ watching television
_____ reading magazines _____ reading novels
_____ surfing the Internet _____ working
_____ talking on the phone _____ pursuing other hobbies

What does the ranking tell you about your priorities regarding God's Word?

_____

If your time spent meditating on God's Word ranks low on your list, how will you determine when God is speaking to you? The more time you spend in the Word of God, the clearer the separation will become between your own desires and what the Holy Spirit is telling you.

Most of us feel we don't have enough time to meditate on God's Word. We all need to purposefully carve out time to spend with God. Here's a simple starting place. Take one or two verses a week and write them on an index card. Stick them to your bathroom mirror or, like my sister Chrystal, to the steering wheel in your car.

Every morning for seven days let these verses be on your heart and mind as you wash your face, brush your teeth, and prepare to start your day. Ask the Lord to speak to you and teach you through His Word as you meditate on it all day long. Consciously bring this verse to your mind as you take part in your daily activities. Ask the Lord to show you how the verses apply to practical scenarios you face. By the end of the week you will have these verses inscribed on your heart and mind.

> Those who do not believe God speaks specifically will simply ignore or explain away the times when God communicates with them. However, those who spend each day in the profound awareness that God does speak are in a wonderful position to receive his Word.[2]
> —Henry and Richard Blackaby

Choose two of the following verses to meditate on this week. Write them on a card and display them where you will see them often.

Psalm 25:14 Psalm 27:13-14 Isaiah 33:6
Zephaniah 3:17 Romans 8:35-37 Galatians 5:1

What has the Holy Spirit taught you as you studied today?

_____

_____

What is God asking you to do as a result of today's study?

_____

_____

Write a prayer responding to God's commands to you.

_____

_____

_____

_____

---

1. Bruce Wilkinson, *Secrets of the Vine* (Sisters, OR: Multnomah Publishers, 2001), 108.
2. Henry and Richard Blackaby, *Hearing God's Voice* (Nashville: Broadman and Holman, 2002), 53.

Day 5 AUTHORITATIVE

I was having a time of prayer during a regular quiet time on a regular morning. I talked with God about the details of my life. I asked Him to allow me to clearly hear His voice throughout the day. As I sat in the presence of God, the name of a friend came to my mind. She was a dear friend yet our lives had drifted apart. I thought of her for a moment and then tried to continue with the task at hand. Again, her name rang like a bell deep inside. Assuming the Lord must be bringing her to my mind for a reason, I offered her and her family to the Lord in prayer.

Then, suddenly, God spoke. *Call her. She needs you.* I sat still for a moment debating the validity of what I had heard. Again, *Call her. She needs you.* Although the message seemed to be of little significance, the impression it made was staggering. My heart sensed the warm stirring that accompanies the voice of God.

I got up and dialed her number. She sounded rushed and frustrated when she answered the phone. Her husband was at work, her babysitter had called in sick, and she was at home with all three of her small children while having to contend with her full-time job that she did from her home office. In addition, there was a mound of clean laundry sitting on her couch.

HE SPEAKS

They said to one another, "Were not our hearts burning within us while He was speaking to us on the road, while He was explaining the Scriptures to us?" Luke 24:32

I spent my quiet time that morning folding a friend's laundry. The voice of the Holy Spirit has an authority that can only come from God. While your conscience may seek to reason and rationalize, God voice comes with such force and weight that it makes a resonating impact on your human conscience.

 God's voice comes with such force and weight that it makes a

resonating impact on my _____ _____.

Read Matthew 7:28-29 and answer the following questions.

What reaction did Jesus' words produce in the hearers?

_____

Why did the hearers react this way? _____

To what group of people is Jesus' teaching contrasted?

_____

The religious leaders of the day could only teach what they had been taught. Jesus needed no references or footnotes to assert the validity of His message. It was self-authenticating and produced automatic awe in those who heard it because it had the authority that can only come from the one true God.

Like the scribes of Jesus' day, our own human conscience will seek to reason with us and explain the "why" by presenting factual evidence to support its decision. When the Holy Spirit speaks, His words come with such sudden, passionate authority that they will produce a holy amazement in you. The authority of His message will strike your inner man with such a blow that it will shake loose your old agenda and replace it with His new one.

THE BURNING HEART

In Luke 24 we read about two men who traveled to Emmaus discussing the current events of the day: Jesus' trial, crucifixion, and burial. They were so engrossed in their conversation that when Jesus joined their caravan they didn't even recognize He was the One whom they were discussing. These men were with Jesus and didn't even know it.

When Jesus began to speak to the men, their hearts started to burn. His words carried an authority and weight that rang in their hearts and amazed them.

Look up each of the following verses and paraphrase Jeremiah's thoughts on the authority of God's Word.

Jeremiah 20:8-9 _____

Jeremiah 23:29 _____

Describe a time when God's voice was clearly evident because of the impact His message had in you.

_____

How did this differ from other voices?

_____

When God speaks, a calm and steady force accompanies His Word and impacts your soul. While your mind will work to rationalize and convince, God's voice simply speaks and its effectiveness conveys His authority.

What has the Holy Spirit taught you as you studied today?

_____

_____

What is God asking you to do as a result of today's study?

_____

_____

Write a prayer responding to God's commands to you.

_____

_____

_____

_____

∽ THIS WEEK AT A GLANCE ∽

Write the key principles from this week's study:

Day 1: _____

_____

Day 2: _____

_____

Day 3: _____

_____

Day 4: _____

_____

Day 5: _____

_____

Look back at your notes from the end of each day of study. List three things the Holy Spirit has encouraged you to do as a result of this week's study.

1. _____

2. _____

3. _____

What immediate steps will you take to respond in obedience?

_____

_____

_____

_____

GOD'S VOICE REVEALS HIS CHARACTER

With all my heart I have sought You;
Do not let me wander from Your commandments.
Open my eyes, that I may behold
Wonderful things from Your law.
Psalm 119:10,18

We get to know God through His written _____ to us.

The better you _____ God, the more clearly you can _____ God.

Focus on _____—not merely on _____ God.

You can distinguish God's voice by _____ _____ Him.

2 Chronicles 16:9—*For the eyes of the* LORD *range throughout the earth to show Himself strong*
for those whose _____.

Don't go _____ hunting instead of _____ hunting.

Correct communion with God _____ can only emanate from intimate
communion with Him _____.

Search the Scripture to get to _____ God, not just to get _____ God.

It is _____ responsibility to cause you to _____ and to _____ His voice.

God leads perfectly because He is _____ and He is _____.

God's Voice Reveals His Character

Day 1   GOD REVEALING

HE SPEAKS
The LORD revealed Himself to Samuel at Shiloh by the word of the LORD.
1 Samuel 3:21

WHOEVER SEEKS GOD AS A MEANS *toward desired ends will not find God. The mighty God, the maker of heaven and earth, will not be one of many treasures, not even the chief of all treasures. He will be all in all or He will be nothing. God will not be used. His mercy and grace are infinite and His patient understanding is beyond measure, but He will not aid men in their selfish striving after personal gain. He will not help men to attain ends which, when attained, usurp the place He by every right should hold in their interest and affection.*[1] —A.W. Tozer

John 16:14, NLT
[The Holy Spirit] will bring me glory by revealing to you whatever he receives from me.

One of God's greatest desires is to make Himself known to us and lead us into a more intimate relationship with Him. Throughout the Bible He demonstrates His desire to have a friendship with us. He is not as much interested in us reaching our destination as He is in the knowledge of Him we gain while we are on the journey. He wants us to know Him.

According to John 16:14, what is the Holy Spirit's goal in revealing

the Father's will to us? _____

The Holy Spirit has one main goal: to bring glory to God the Father and the Son by revealing the Father's thoughts concerning us.

The Holy Spirit's primary goal is to _____ God the

Father and the Son by revealing the _____ thoughts.

KNOW GOD NOT JUST HIS DIRECTION

Often we seek to know God's direction more than we seek to know God. We bypass the relationship because we would rather have answers about us. God wants to speak to you because He wants you to know Him; knowing His direction is just a by-product. God seeks to reveal truth about Himself because this knowledge will lay the firm path you can walk to fulfilling God's purpose for your life.

Does your request to hear God's voice revolve mostly around:
○ your desire to know what God wants you to do?
○ your desire to know where God wants you to go?
○ your desire to know God?

Hearing from God will always be designed to point you to Him and open up your understanding and your experience concerning who He is. Without knowledge of the nature of God, obedience to Him becomes more difficult, if not impossible. The more you know and believe to be true about who God is and what He can do, the more willing you become to obey what He commands.

You can separate any other voice from God's by asking these questions:
- Does what I am hearing reveal to me some truth about the character and nature of God?
- Will obedience to this directive cause me to discover and experience an aspect of God's character?

When the Enemy speaks to you he will distort the character and Word of God. Anything that doesn't reflect the character of God is not a message from Him.

> The more you know and believe to be true about who God is and what He can do, the more willing you become to obey what He commands.

FROM THE MIND TO THE HEART

When God instructs us to do something based on our knowledge of Him, He moves our relationship from mental to experiential. This is why He so passionately desires to reveal Himself to us through His Word. God doesn't just want us to hear about Him but to see and experience Him in our lives. We move from knowledge *about* God to experience *with* God when He reveals a characteristic; we then experience that characteristic as we step out in obedience to Him.

I know
the Lord is
speaking to
me when
what I hear
and am led
to do can-
not be done
without His
assistance,
protection and
guidance.
He only
speaks what
brings glory
to Himself!
—Bishop
Kenneth Ulmer

Record what God revealed about Himself in each passage and the circumstances in their lives that made this knowledge necessary.

Moses—Exodus 34:6-7 _____

_____

Malachi —Malachi 3:6-7 _____

_____

Without this knowledge of the nature of God, obedience to Him would have been more difficult, if not impossible. The more you believe about who God is and what He is able to do, the more willing you will be to obey what He asks.

Nancy and Jeff were victims of Hurricane Katrina. The storms completely destroyed their home. With dwindling savings and limited resources at their disposal, they still felt blessed considering the many people who lost family members in the storm. Despite their loss, they sensed God leading them to help take care of families who had lost loved ones instead of being taken care of themselves. It didn't seem rational to extend themselves to others when they were in need, but this persistent leading continued to permeate their thoughts. As they sought God in prayer and Bible study, the attribute of His unfailing love seemed to be a recurring theme.

They determined that doing what God was leading them to do, no matter how crazy it appeared to others, would enable them to experience the love of God in a personal way. So they moved forward in obedience to assist the thousands displaced by the storm. As a result, they experienced God's incredible love for them in unimaginable ways—from free housing to job opportunities. This couple *experienced* God's love in a way they never had before.

Job 42:5
I have heard of You
by the hearing
of the ear;
But now my eye
sees You.

List two characteristics of God that you have experienced in the

past month. _____

How did your obedience foster this experience? Be prepared to discuss this with your small group.

_____

During the week, do an Internet search on the names of God. His names signify His character. Read and familiarize yourself with some of the names of God and their meanings. Pick one or two that mean the most to you to share with your small group.

What has the Holy Spirit taught you as you studied today?

_____

_____

What is God asking you to do as a result of today's study?

_____

_____

_____

Write a prayer responding to God's commands to you.

_____

_____

_____

_____

---

1. A. W. Tozer, *Man: The Dwelling Place of God* (Harrisburg, PA: Christian Publications, 1966), 57.

Day 2 LOVING

THIS MESSAGE—I AM SOMEONE *God so loves*—is a *message we're likely to hear from God in contemplation ... God is so anxious to tell us this that the only time God is pictured in a hurry in Scripture is when the father ran down the trail to the prodigal son, "threw his arms around him and kissed him."*[1]
—*Jan Johnson*

HE SPEAKS
There is now no condemnation for those who are in Christ Jesus.
Romans 8:1

My college years took me from the sheltered life of my Christian family to another world. I was both overwhelmed and excited by the lifestyle before me. However, I soon found myself living contrary to what I knew would please the Lord. As a result, in the years that followed my undergraduate education I struggled with guilt about the things I had done.

No matter what I accomplished or how far I removed myself from the life-style choices I had made, a nagging voice in my head always kept pouring on the guilt. I wondered why I was continually reminded about my past and allowed to experience the accompanying guilt.

As I struggled with this I ran across a verse that spoke to my heart: "Do not call to mind the former things, or ponder things of the past. Behold I will do something new" (Isa. 43:18-19). The Lord reminded me that He seeks to deliver me from the guilt of the past and move me toward the promise of the future. His goal is never to bring guilt and condemnation by continually reminding me of my past sins but rather to bring healing and obedience by turning my attention to my future with Him.

 God seeks to deliver me from the guilt of the _____

and move me toward the promise of the _____.

The Holy Spirit reveals the character of God to us. According to 1 John 4:8, "God is love." It's who He is and what He invites all of us to experience.

Look up 1 Corinthians 13:4-8 and list in the margin the words and phrases that describe God's love.

How do those terms help you distinguish between God's convicting voice and the Enemy's condemning voice?

_____

> God's aim is always to lovingly steer us in the direction of His grace.

God doesn't point out our sin to condemn us. God's purpose in lovingly revealing our sin is to encourage us to acknowledge it and confess it so He can change us. The Enemy's voice brings condemnation. You will know condemnation because it will bring guilt and offer no clear means of relief. On the other hand, the Holy Spirit brings conviction that always provides a road map out and away from a specific sin. His aim is always to lovingly steer us in the direction of His grace.

What words of condemnation have you struggled with and wondered whether or not they came from God?

_____

Offer these words of condemnation to God in prayer. Tell Him you now recognize these words are not from Him. As you do, cross through each word to symbolize your decision not to let these thoughts govern your thinking.

NO CONDEMNATION

In John 8, Pharisees brought into the temple a woman caught in the act of adultery. These men revealed her sin, sought to expose her, and embarrassed her before the crowd. Can you imagine how she must have felt with her sin exposed not just to the religious Pharisees but to everyone in the temple? Imagine someone catching you in some lewd sin and dragging you to a Bible study at your church where all your friends are gathered. These men didn't seek to restore her. They just wanted to embarrass and expose her. This is Satan's goal as well.

They brought her to Jesus, and He said, "He who is without sin among you, let him be the first to throw a stone at her" (v. 7). The only person qualified was the Speaker, but He didn't throw the stone. What a great truth. God has the right to condemn us, but He has chosen not to throw stones. He bestows grace and love despite what we have done, because His very nature is love.

Whenever I feel the pain of "stones" thrown at me, I quickly realize they didn't come from my Lord. For instance, when I have missed having my quiet time and begin to feel guilty, I recognize this isn't the Lord's attempt to get me back into Bible study and personal time with Him. He doesn't want me to come to Him out of guilt but out of love and affection. I know He is wooing me when I feel a soothing conviction that tenderly urges me to respond to His love.

In what areas do you tend to operate out of guilt rather than love?

_____

Condemn—to judge, to be worthy of punishment

Convict—to convince; to bring to light, to expose and correct

God has chosen not to throw stones.

One by one, the Pharisees realized they would not be able to meet Jesus' qualifications to condemn this woman, so they left. Then Jesus spoke.

Read John 8:11 (margin) and underline Jesus' two main points.

He doesn't dismiss or make excuses for her sin; He just doesn't condemn her for it. His voice will always point out sin but offer grace to continue on in righteousness. He doesn't bring up the past without pointing toward the future.

When God speaks to us, His words will not heap judgment on us. He reveals our sins to lead us to repentance, but this revelation is buffered with the hope of His grace, love, and another chance. He has already undergone the punishment for our sin once and for all on the cross.

John 8:11
Jesus said, "I do not condemn you, either. Go. From now on sin no more."

Isaiah 54:4
Fear not, for you will not be put to shame; And do not feel humiliated, for you will not be disgraced; But you will forget the shame of your youth, And the reproach of your widowhood you will remember no more.

Condemnation offers only guilt and judgment as it points out the problem; the soothing conviction of God offers a solution. You will know God's voice because it will bring encouragement along with conviction. From the very beginning God sought to speak with His children, revealing sin while restoring relationship.

Describe how God's voice brought both conviction and encouragement in the following examples.

	Conviction	Encouragement
2 Chronicles 7:14		
Isaiah 1:16-18		
Ezekiel 18:30-32		

The purpose of the voice of condemnation is to push you away from His presence —that which is the very source of your victory. The purpose of the voice of conviction is to press you into the face of Christ.[2]
—Bob Sorge

What has the Holy Spirit taught you as you studied today?

_____

_____

What is God asking you to do as a result of today's study?

_____

_____

Write a prayer responding to God's commands to you.

_____

_____

_____

_____

---

1. Jan Johnson, *When the Soul Listens* (Colorado Springs: NavPress, 1999), 156.
2. Bob Sorge, *Secrets of the Secret Place* (Lee's Summit, MO: Oasis House, 2001), 57-58.

Day 3 PEACEFUL

I KNOW GOD IS SPEAKING *to me when, in spite of my initial struggle, an undeniable release and peace follows when I have obeyed His voice. When I finally do the thing He has been nudging me to do, whether it's letting something or someone go, or taking a step toward the unknown, there is a deep calm in my soul. Where my heart and mind were once filled with terrible angst, I am now filled with a supernatural peace.* —Kathy Troccoli

HE SPEAKS
These things I have spoken to you that in me you may have peace.
John 16:33

As a young preacher in Dallas, my father had an internal peace about a vision the Lord had given him for ministry. He believed God wanted his small church to not only own the building where they met but the entire street so that they could serve the community. They had no money to buy the land. Many people in the community and even within the congregation were not on board since it seemed impossible. Still God's peace ruled in Tony Evans' heart. He moved forward in obedience expecting to see God's supernatural activity as a result. Today Oak Cliff Bible Fellowship owns the street on which it sits, many of the businesses on that street, and is able to minister to the community more effectively as a result.

Numbers 6:26
The LORD lift up His countenance on you, And give you peace.

Before Jesus died He offered comforting words to His disciples. He explained that He was leaving His peace with them even when He was gone. His peace would serve as an internal mechanism by which they could discern God's voice.

God's _____ serves as a mechanism by which I can

discern _____   _____.

What are some differences between the peace Jesus gives and what the world can offer?

_____

Peace is a gift that accompanied your salvation. It is one of the great blessings from our Father to His children. It is one of the names of the Holy Spirit that depicts His character.

John 14:27
Peace I leave with
you; My peace
I give to you; not
as the world gives,
do I give to you.
Let not your heart
be troubled, nor
let it be fearful.

The Greek word for *peace* used in John 14:27 is *eirene*. It means to be exempt from rage and havoc of war, to be at rest and quietness. This word is also used to describe peace between individuals. Christ desired for His peace to govern internally and externally. The Holy Spirit lives within us to give us a continually peaceful assurance internally that directs us to make decisions that honor the Lord and guides our relationships with others.

PEACE THAT RULES

**He is Jehovah
Shalom—the
God of Peace.**

God's personal word to you will be accompanied by a sense of assurance and peace. When you sense God's leading ask yourself, *Do I feel confident and peaceful about moving forward or am I restless and unsure about the directions I have received?* Can you move forward in confidence that you will not be betraying yourself?

Even when doing something that seems impossible, God's peace will accompany your actions if it is His will. You may not feel confident in your own ability but you can grow in confidence in His.

Recall a time when you moved forward without a complete green light. What were the results?

_____

Psalm 29:11
The LORD will
bless His people
with peace.

As my husband and I courted and moved toward marriage, I was terrified. I had been in relationships before that had caused me pain. I was fearful about the prospect of committing my life to a man.

After prayer and wise counsel I began to suspect that the Lord was guiding me to marry him, but I had no confidence in my ability to be a wife. The Lord began to give me an unexplained confidence in His ability even though I knew that left to my own devices, I was ill-equipped.

**God graciously
gives us His
peace so He
can demon-
strate His
supernatural
activity in
our lives.**

God graciously gives us His peace so He can demonstrate His supernatural activity in our lives. You may feel ill-equipped to handle many things God calls you to do, but when you sense His peace He is encouraging you to step out in obedience. When you obey, you will experience His supernatural power operating through you to do it.

Read Colossians 3:15 and fill in the blanks.

Let the _____ of Christ _____
in your hearts.

When we obey God, we experience internal tranquility. When we step outside of the will of God, we feel uneasy. Our God-given peace cannot be lost; but if something is not pleasing to God, peace will not rule.

When we feel a tug of war ensuing in our hearts, we need to pay close attention; God is speaking. When we know the Holy Spirit is leading us in a particular direction, to go against that leading is, in essence, to reject the leading of the Holy Spirit and sin against God.

Colossians 3:15 says that the peace of God should rule our hearts, not our circumstances. We can't depend on what our circumstances say to determine what God is doing. We must always look inward first and move according to the Holy Spirit's witness in accordance with God's Word. When peace rules in our hearts we can confidently move forward regardless of what external circumstances look or feel like and regardless of what others say.

Job 22:21
Yield now and be at peace with Him.

Refer to the front or back cover of this book where you listed the life situations about which you are trying to discern God's leading. Place a star beside those you sense God's peace is ruling and a circle beside those it is not.

Are you moving forward in obedience in those areas you sense God's ruling peace? Are you moving forward prematurely in the areas where you don't?

2 Timothy 1:7
God has not given us a spirit of timidity but of power and love and discipline.

What has the Holy Spirit taught you as you studied today?

_____

_____

_____

What is God asking you to do as a result of today's study?

_____

_____

Write a prayer responding to God's commands to you.

_____

_____

_____

_____

Day 4   TRUTHFUL

HE SPEAKS

The word of the LORD holds true and everything he does is worthy of our trust.
Psalm 33:4, NLT

I KNOW THE LORD IS SPEAKING *to me when what I think He is saying is driven home by Scripture! Once when wondering whether to get myself into some pubs in England to talk to the kids there, I subconsciously worried about my reputation. What would people think if they saw me going in those places? As I sought to find what was the "right" not the "comfortable" thing to do, I read in Philippians 2, "[He] made Himself of no reputation." The still voice said to my soul, "What are you worrying about your reputation for?" I went. —Jill Briscoe*

As Tara and I conversed about her decision to move in with her unsaved boyfriend, my patience grew thin. She had woven a web of rationalizations to excuse her actions that even included Scripture references taken out of context. She was certain she had heard from God and He was not only allowing but blessing her union with this young man. I thought back to when Tara accepted Christ and the spiritual fruit her salvation had produced. Knowing the Holy Spirit indwelled her, I wondered how she could now be so off base about God's voice.

We have all been in this position at one time or another. Different circumstances; same dilemma. How can we hear God clearly and discern His voice from the Enemy's or even from the voices of our own egos?

Complete the sentence below. Check your answer by looking back at page 66. The Holy Spirit's primary goal is:

_____

The more acquainted you become with God, the more clearly you will identify His word. His tone is love while the Accuser's is guilt and condemnation. God's voice is peace while the Enemy's is fear and chaos.

Another distinguishing characteristic of God's voice is truthfulness. He cannot and will never lie. His spoken word will never contradict His character revealed in His written Word. He will never cause you to sin, steer you outside of His will, or encourage you to cover your sin.

When God speaks I can be certain it will be _____.

Read John 16:13 in the margin. What causes the Holy Spirit to reveal truth to God's people?

_____

_____

Every message the Spirit delivers comes straight from the God of Truth. Only the Holy Spirit has direct access to God's thoughts. He lives in you and desires to share these revelations with those who will listen.

Tara might have felt led to make the decisions she had chosen, but she wasn't being led by the Holy Spirit. What she heard clearly misrepresented the standards set by God in His Word.

Choose two of the statements below and describe why each misrepresents God's truth. Add any Scripture you come across that validates your response. I've helped you out on a few of them. Be prepared to discuss this with your small group and add to this list.

- I don't need to be part of a local church (Heb. 10:25).
- I don't like the decision my husband is making. I refuse to follow him in this matter (Eph. 5:22-23).
- I'm a Christian, but I feel unworthy. I know God doesn't hear me when I pray (Mic. 7:7; Heb. 10:22).
- I don't make enough money to tithe right now. God understands (Mal. 3:8-10).

1. _____

_____

2. _____

_____

MY TRUTH IS NOT THE TRUTH OF GOD

Further conversation with Tara revealed a family legacy of women who lived with men before marriage. My goal in our conversation was to help her realize that family traditions, no matter how deeply woven into the fabric of her life, don't override the truth of God.

What personal beliefs have you allowed to override God's truth?

_____

_____

John 16:13
When He, the Spirit of truth, comes, He will guide you into all the truth; for He will not speak on His own initiative, but whatever He hears, He will speak; and He will disclose to you what is to come.

1 Corinthians 2:10-12
The Spirit searches all things, even the depths of God. For who among men knows the thoughts of a man except the spirit of the man which is in him? Even so the thoughts of God no one knows except the Spirit of God. Now we have received, not the spirit of the world, but the Spirit who is from God, so that we may know the things freely given to us by God.

God's standard of truth may differ from the standard of your family, denomination, or culture. Just because we feel comfortable doing something doesn't make it right. We must filter it through the truth of God. His Word is truth and when His Spirit speaks, He will only speak truth.

❧ ASSURED BY HIS TRUTH ❧

God's assurance accompanies His truth. When He speaks, He will do everything He says. His promises are not empty. When you choose to rely on God's standards over your own and follow His leading in obedience, you will see the glorious results that only come when we rely on the truth and righteous standard of God.

The more acquainted you are with God's Word, the more accurately you will be able to hear Him. In a world singed with sin and pride, it is difficult to be certain when God is speaking. However, since the Word of God provides the framework into which His messages to us will fall and is in itself the chief means through which He speaks, we can be certain to hear God most clearly when we remain consistent in our study of and meditation on His Word.

Psalm 119:9, NLT
How can a young person stay pure? By obeying your words and following its rules.

What has the Holy Spirit taught you as you studied today?

_____

_____

_____

Titus 1:2
God ... cannot lie.

What is God asking you to do as a result of today's study?

_____

_____

Write a prayer responding to God's commands to you.

_____

_____

_____

_____

Day 5 POWERFUL

I KNOW THE LORD IS SPEAKING *to me when I carefully consider the spirit, the quality, and the content of the voice I am hearing. The spirit of the voice of God is a spirit of gentleness. It is the Spirit of Jesus. When He speaks, He will not crush the needy or snuff out hope. The quality of His voice is one that draws and encourages rather than one that pushes and condemns. The content of His voice will be consistent with what He has already revealed in Scripture. That is why we must know Scripture. He will never contradict Himself.*
—*Richard Foster*

HE SPEAKS

The voice of the LORD echoes above the sea. The God of glory thunders. The LORD thunders above the mighty sea. The voice of the LORD is powerful; the voice of the LORD is full of majesty.
Psalm 29:3-4

The waves crashed against the side of the boat with tremendous power and strength. This was supposed to be a dream family vacation, but it was turning into a nightmare. The cruise had gone well up until this point, but now we were right in the middle of a storm. My siblings and I nestled into my parents' cabin and huddled near the window. I will never forget what I saw. The 40-foot waves dashed against the side of the boat and seemed to toss it around like it was a small wooden canoe. As far as I could see there was only water and we were at its mercy. The sea possessed an authority and command beyond my comprehension. Our captain, our ship, and our lives all seemed to be at its disposal.

God used the force of those waves that day to teach me a lesson about His voice. When God speaks, He does so with power and authority. If the waters have that much control, then how much more the voice of God that commands the water itself! When God speaks, things change.

 When God speaks, He does so with _____

and _____.

He is Jehovah Elohim — the God who can create something out of nothing.

He is Jehovah Elohim—the God who can create something out of nothing. Do we believe there is enough power in God's voice to do these kinds of things in our lives right now? Instead of looking at scriptural examples as exceptions to the rule, consider them examples divinely given to reveal what God can and will do today.

God's powerful voice:
- created the waters (Genesis 1:7)
- divided the water from the dry land (Genesis 1:9)
- produced a human being out of dust (Genesis 2:7)
- imposed order out of chaos (Genesis 1)
- spoke peace to a storm, bringing complete peace (Luke 8:24)
- raised Lazarus from the grave (John 11:43)
- caused the Enemy to flee (Matthew 4:11)
- called a woman out from her hiding place (Luke 7:37)
- instantly forgave sin (John 8:11)

Carefully read through the list in the margin. Look at the verb in each. Which describe what you need the powerful voice of the Lord to do in your life?

_____

_____

What sources other than God's voice have you been seeking?

_____

_____

God's voice alone has the authority to accomplish what we need. As we recognize the power of God's voice we will be more willing to seek it, wait for it, and submit to it. We won't spend so much time and energy seeking answers outside of God's will.

THE CHARACTERISTICS OF HIS VOICE

In Luke 8, Jesus speaks to the winds and waves and calls them to peace. Verse 24 says, "They stopped, and it became calm."

One way we distinguish God's voice from others is in the effect it has on our circumstances. When Jesus calmed the waves, the response was immediate. It didn't take a series of follow-up commands or help from the disciples to stop the raging waters. One word from Jesus and things changed on the spot. Of course, this is not always the case. Many times God will sovereignly take us on a journey to the fulfillment of His word to us, but whether the result is instant or gradual, God shows His authority.

Matthew had been married for five years when his marriage began to struggle. He took his concerns to the Lord and asked Him to supernaturally infiltrate his circumstances. While searching the Scripture, Matthew was reminded of how God had given His life for him even when he didn't deserve it. He knew God was asking him to love his wife the same way he was loved by God: unconditionally and completely. Matthew asked the Lord to allow him to see his wife through the Lord's eyes. He emerged from his time with the Lord and noticed a change. His wife was the same, his marriage was the same, but he was different. God's voice had changed him. He saw his wife in a brand new way. Thirty-five years later, this couple testifies to the changing power of God's Word.

Often when things in our lives change we attribute the transformation to something other than God's voice. We assume all our hard work finally paid off.

On the contrary, when we see things changing, we should consider that God is up to something.

We can recognize the fact that God has spoken when obvious change points us to focus our attention God-ward. When the disciples saw the effect Jesus' word had on the water, they were "fearful and amazed" (Luke 8:25). They saw Him in a new way after they experienced the power of His spoken word in their lives.

> Recall a time when God's word produced change in your life. How did this change bring glory to God? Be prepared to share this with your small group.

_____

_____

What has the Holy Spirit taught you as you studied today?

_____

_____

_____

What is God asking you to do as a result of today's study?

_____

_____

_____

Write a prayer responding to God's commands to you.

_____

_____

_____

_____

THIS WEEK AT A GLANCE

Write the key principles from this week's study:

Day 1: _____

_____

Day 2: _____

_____

Day 3: _____

_____

Day 4: _____

_____

Day 5: _____

_____

Look back at your notes from the end of each day of study. List three things the Holy Spirit has encouraged you to do as a result of this week's study.

1. _____

2. _____

3. _____

What immediate steps will you take to respond in obedience?

_____

_____

_____

_____

GOD'S VOICE REVEALS HIS PLAN

*We are His creation—created in Christ Jesus for good works which God
prepared ahead of time so that we should walk in them.*
Ephesians 2:10, HCSB

Our God doesn't just sit on _____ and look down _____.

Five Principles about God's Plan for Your Life

1. God's plan is often _____ while you are in the _____

_____ of your life.

2. You are _____ for God's plan while you are in the desert:

Moses was:

A. equipped with _____

B. equipped with _____

C. equipped with _____

3. _____ _____ will point you to God's plan.

4. _____ _____ is the purpose of God's plan.

5. God's plan _____ of your life.

God's Voice Reveals His Plan

Day 1   GOD'S PURPOSEFUL VOICE

HE SPEAKS
We are His workmanship, created in Christ Jesus for good works, which He prepared beforehand so that we might walk in them.
Ephesians 2:10

NOTHING PLEASES GOD MORE *than when we ask for what He wants to give. When we spend time with Him and allow his priorities, passion, and purposes to motivate us, we will ask for things that are closest to His Heart.[1] —Bruce Wilkinson*

My pastor said to me, "I want you to coordinate the women's conference at our church." The spirit of the women in our fellowship seemed to be waning. We lacked a thirst to deepen our relationship with the Lord. This became evident as fewer and fewer women participated in programs designed specifically for spiritual growth.

I felt thrilled that God would allow me to try to restart the engines of their hearts with a Bible-teaching worship conference. I appointed a committee and started plans to put together an event for the women of our congregation. My goal was to target the women of my home church and only open the event to them.

When word got out to the community, we began to receive calls from women's ministries everywhere, even other cities and states. My initial reaction was to overlook their interest and remained focused on my goal, which only included our women. But the calls kept coming.

We realized that women outside our church needed what we were offering. We had already spent months planning the event. We weren't prepared to handle an influx of visitors, but I went back to the drawing board to seek God in prayer. Maybe God's plans and purposes were different than mine. The committee needed to go where He was obviously leading.

The conference is four years old now, and each year about 3,500 women gather from every denomination, race, and age to spend a couple of days in the presence of God. His purposes were so much bigger than mine. What a great ministry opportunity we would have missed had I ignored God's plans and purposes while selfishly pursuing my own! This event led me to search my heart: As I seek to hear God's voice, do I *really* desire to hear what His purposes are, or do I just desire to pursue my own and hope for His blessing?

What do you desire most?
○ to know God's plans and adjust my life to fit with them
○ to proceed with my plans and hope God will bless them

Last week we learned about funneling what we hear from the Holy Spirit through God's character as revealed in His Word. We also have to funnel it through the purposes of God. He will never speak a word to you that will contradict His character or His sovereignly designed plans.

God's word will not contradict His _____ or

His _____ _____ plans.

Before we can accurately discern God's voice we have to recognize and believe that *God has a plan.* He has written a script we are to follow. He doesn't want us to create our own, write new lines, or change His to suit our agendas. He just wants us to recognize and trust that His plans are best.

God's plans were formulated and prepared before your birth or even before time began. He already has an agenda for your career, ministry, finances, and family; and His plans should always take precedence over your own!

We have to decide either to spend our time discovering and aligning ourselves with the purposes of God or doing what we want while asking God to bless it. I have often plowed ahead with my purposes hoping God would give them His seal of approval.

What have you learned that might help you avoid the trap
of proceeding with your own plans and asking God to bless
the result?

_____

_____

Believing that God is in ultimate control and has a sovereign plan governing our lives gives us a framework through which to understand God's leading. Without confident trust in this biblical truth, we will lack the means to clearly hear God's voice speaking to us.

Think of a difficult situation you're currently facing. Do you really want to know God's will regarding that situation?
○ yes ○ no ○ not sure

Do you really believe God already has a plan for you in that situation?
○ yes ○ no ○ not sure

Are you willing to submit your agenda to His?
○ yes ○ no ○ not sure

John 7:17, NLT
Anyone who wants to do the will of God will know [it].

Look up the following references and describe how each confirms that God has a plan we are to follow.

Deuteronomy 5:32-33 _____

_____

Psalm 81:13-14 _____

_____

❧ THE PURPOSES OF GOD ❧

"We are God's masterpiece. He has created us anew in Christ Jesus, so that we can do the good things he planned for us long ago" (Eph. 2:10, NLT). Let's look closely at the details of this verse as we discover how significant the plans of God are for our lives.

This verse makes four powerful points. You are (1) a masterpiece; (2) created anew; (3) to do good things; and (4) to act according to His plan. The King James Version calls us God's workmanship. The New Living Translation uses the word *masterpiece*, which more clearly paints the picture Paul described. He wanted us to recognize we are priceless works of art in the eyes of our Master.

We are priceless works of art in the eyes of our Master.

Secondly, God re-created us fully equipped in Christ to handle what God's will requires and to do good works. Since we are to participate in works that have been prepared beforehand, we can't accomplish them in our own power.

We walk in them as Christ expresses Himself in and through us. God created us anew to walk in His divinely-created purposes.

As we seek to hear God's voice and discover His plan, we must believe that He has a sovereign plan for our lives. When He speaks, His voice will always be in accordance with His purposes.

What has the Holy Spirit taught you as you studied today?

_____

_____

_____

What is God asking you to do as a result of today's study?

_____

_____

_____

Write a prayer responding to God's commands to you.

_____

_____

_____

_____

_____

_____

_____

_____

1. Bruce Wilkinson, *Secrets of the Vine* (Sisters, OR: Multnomah Publishers, 2001), 115.

Day 2 GOD'S INVITATIONAL VOICE

HE SPEAKS
Jesus said to him,
"Follow Me."
John 1:43

God makes His desires known to those who stop at His Word, look in with a sensitive spirit, and listen to others. When we go to His Word, we stop long enough to hear from above. When we look, we examine our surrounding circumstances in light of what He is saying to our inner spirit (perhaps you prefer to call this your conscience). And when we listen to others, we seek the counsel of wise, qualified people.[1] —Charles R. Swindoll

My friend Kimberly is a mother of four. Years ago she was looking for an opportunity to work in ministry. In Bible study and through the leading of the Spirit, she sensed the Lord leading her to minister to women. Her ultimate desire was to speak to women across the country in conference settings.

She prayerfully offered these desires to the Lord for several years and was disappointed when she didn't receive many invitations to speak at events. Kimberly even created a brochure on her ministry and sent it to local churches. She never received a response.

Meanwhile, Kimberly's 16-year-old daughter had lots of friends who visited their home. During their get-togethers they often engaged her in conversation that led to spiritual matters. While Kimberly had quiet time with the Lord one morning, He showed her His plan. God wanted her to minister to this group of young women.

While Kimberly was frantically trying to create ministry opportunities, she had missed seeing God's plan. When her eyes were opened to what God was doing, she immediately stopped her plan and began to follow His. Now Kimberly has a flourishing ministry to young women. Each week, dozens of young girls show up at her home to listen to her teach God's Word.

When you see evidence that God is moving, take it as your cue to jump on board and join Him. The Holy Spirit reveals God's plan to us as He orchestrates the circumstances of our lives. When our spiritual eyes are open to see His divine activity on earth, He has *allowed* us to see them as a way to personally invite us to participate with Him.

🌸 **The Holy Spirit reveals _____ _____ to me**

as He orchestrates the _____ of my life.

What circumstances led to Samuel's meeting with Saul in

1 Samuel 9:1-15? _____

Romans 8:28
We know that God causes all things to work together for good to those who love God, to those who are called according to His purpose.

Even seemingly meaningless activities are used by God as a tool to guide us toward His plans. Never think your circumstances are disconnected from God's leading and His will. Don't spend your time wishing you could get out of the season of life you are in; rather, spend your time looking fervently for God's hand in your situation.

When seeking God's guidance, always take into account the activity He is allowing in your life at that time. The Enemy's discouraging voice tells us what we could do "if." The voice of God tells us what we should do now. When you ask God for direction, keep your eyes open to see what He does next.

Look back at the life situations you wrote inside the front or back cover of your book. How do you see God moving in these areas?

_____

What does this confirm about how you should proceed?

_____

About a year ago, a friend sent me a book about silent prayer. The book helped explain how purposeful periods of silent prayer can assist a believer in hearing from God. I was very drawn to the book and the spiritual journey the author described.

I read the book twice and knew the Lord was calling me to experience Him in prayer in a brand-new way. Not long after my first reading of the book, my personal Bible study led me to Ecclesiastes 5:1-2, "As you enter into the house of God, keep your ears open and your mouth shut! ... let your words be few" (NLT). It connected with the message of the book and confirmed what I sensed the Holy Spirit was leading me to do.

Several days later I was in a meeting when someone mentioned an upcoming retreat that some ladies in our church were taking. It was a silent retreat. Women would gather for the purpose of spending 36 hours in silence, anticipating God's voice. I had never heard of such a thing. The circumstances of my life confirmed the direction God was leading me. I knew He was speaking.

Recall a time when the circumstances of your life confirmed God's leading and steered you in His direction. Be prepared to share this with your small group.

_____

_____

God confirmed my direction while I attended a necessary but mundane meeting. We often find God's will when we do what's next and obediently respond to the normal duties of life. Elisabeth Elliot said that one of the best pieces of advice she ever got was "Do the next thing."[2] We encounter God's guidance as we engage in the usual activities of life.

God is the God of right now. He calls us not to be regretful over yesterday or worried about tomorrow. He wants us to focus on what He is saying to us and putting in front of us right now. The Enemy's voice will focus on the past and the future while the voice of our God will focus on today. He is the God of right now.

What's the next step for you?

_____

FOLLOW ME

One of the clearest ways to discern God's voice is to ask Him to open your spiritual eyes to see His activity. When we see it, we need to immediately desert what we are doing to join Him. When God allows you to see His activity in the circumstances of your life, you have heard the voice of God.

John 12:26

If anyone serves Me, he must follow Me; and where I am, there My servant will be also.

Read John 12:26 in the margin. Underline the two things this verse reveals about God's true servants.

The principles of this passage strongly convict me. True servants of God follow Him and go where He goes. When God speaks to us, He often does so by allowing us to see His movement; this is an effort to show us His purposes and invite us to participate in them.

Jesus Himself gave the most perfect example of the principle of invitation. Paraphrase John 5:19 below.

_____

_____

Jesus demonstrated how the Father invites us to participate in His work. The beauty of Jesus' life on earth is not only that He did His Father's will but that *He did His Father's will and nothing else.* He didn't create new ideas or strike out on His own.

I suspect we often don't experience the results we desire because we haven't waited for our invitation. We have invited ourselves to do things that God isn't doing.

God *wants* to reveal Himself and His plans to you. He isn't trying to keep you from discovering His will. Look around you. Ask God to open your eyes so you can see what He is up to and then quickly join in.

What has the Holy Spirit taught you as you studied today?

_____

_____

_____

What is God asking you to do as a result of today's study?

_____

_____

_____

Write a prayer responding to God's commands to you.

_____

_____

_____

_____

_____

_____

1. Charles R. Swindoll, "Struggling with God's Will," in *Ten Answers to Life's Most Perplexing Problems,* ed. John Van Diest (Sisters, OR: Multnomah, 1998), 242.
2. Elisabeth Elliot, *A Slow and Certain Light* (Waco, TX: Wordbooks, 1973), 87.

GOD'S TIMELY VOICE

Day 3

HE SPEAKS

There is an appointed time for everything. And there is a time for every event under heaven ... a time to be silent and a time to speak.

Ecclesiastes 3:1,7

My acceptance of his timing was a rigorous exercise in trust. I was tempted to charge the Lord with negligence and inattention, like the disciples in the boat in a storm. They toiled frantically until the situation became impossible and then instead of asking for Jesus' help they yelled, "Master, don't you care that we're drowning?" They weren't perishing, they were panicking. It was not too late. Jesus got up and merely spoke to the wind and sea.[2]

—Elisabeth Elliot

THIS THIEF'S VOICE, UNLIKE GOD'S *voice, threatens and intimidates on the basis of fear:* If you don't do this, you'll be sorry. *It may order you or try to force you to do things. It is often urgent and pressing, sermonizing and demeaning:* Do this now! If you wait, all will be lost![1] *—Jan Johnson*

God has invited you to join Him in His plans. The purposes of God not only include specific plans but also very specific timing. He orchestrates both events in your life and their timing. When He speaks it will be in His perfect timing to accomplish His agenda.

 When He speaks it will be in His _____ _____

to accomplish His _____.

God called Jeremiah to be a prophet while he was very young. Jeremiah thought he was too young (Jer. 1:5-6), but the Lord persisted because the timing fit His agenda. For a century, immoral and sinful kings had ruled with no respect for the things of God. The nation had turned its back on God. Second Kings 23:1-25 records the reformation. King Josiah summoned the national leaders to the temple to burn their idols. God called Jeremiah during this season of national renewal.

God had a plan and the time was ripe for it to be fulfilled. The Master considered the entire scope of His plan when He called the prophet. Jeremiah's obedience combined with national events to accomplish God's grand design.

Time and time again the Lord has shown why He chose to reveal something concerning His will for my life when He did. His timing has often been late as far as I was concerned, but now I see that I would have tried to rush ahead of God instead of waiting for His timing. If He had spoken to me five years ago about the details of the ministry He has entrusted to me now, I either wouldn't have believed the scope of what He had planned or I would have rushed impatiently toward it before I was emotionally and spiritually equipped for the demands I currently face. The timing of the call was just as important as the call itself.

I am learning that God will use the appropriate means to reveal His will in His timing. When it is time for us to know, we will. Much of the heartache and frustration I have encountered in discerning God's voice came because I wanted it before God was ready to give it. I wasn't willing to trust God's timing in revealing His plans for me. I tried to place my time constraints on God.

The Father continues to patiently remind me that His timing is best. Knowing too much too soon can be detrimental. Jesus expressed this to the disciples when He said, "I have many more things to say to you, but you cannot bear them now" (John 16:12).

When airplanes land, their individual flight pattern is not all that matters. The air-traffic controller must consider all the planes in the air and on the ground. When the pilot receives the next instruction depends on all those planes. If a pilot says, "I'm going to land" before receiving instructions from the tower, the results can be disastrous to him and many other people.

How does this analogy apply to waiting on instructions from the Father?

_____

_____

_____

Pilots must learn to wait for directions from someone with a greater perspective. When pilots do receive instructions, they only do as much as they have been instructed to do. Then they wait for more instructions. Each step and the timing of these instructions is crucial to the success of all involved. When God gives you instructions, trust that He has given you what you need for now. He will give more when the time is right.

NO NEED TO HURRY

Nothing takes God off guard. When we feel rushed and hurried to make a decision not rooted in a deep confidence of inner peace, God probably has not spoken. Nowhere in Scripture does God tell anyone to rush into making a decision. On the contrary, He patiently and persistently gives us clarity before requiring obedience. If you feel an overwhelming urge to act spontaneously, pull in the reins.

Read John 10:2-4 in the margin. Underline the portions that clearly characterize the way our Shepherd leads.

One of the things I underlined was He "leads them out." Our Shepherd leads, He doesn't drive. One difference between the Enemy's voice and the Shepherd's is that Jesus doesn't coerce us with fear or intimidation. He gently encourages and woos.

John 10:2-4

He who enters by the door is a shepherd of the sheep. To him the doorkeeper opens, and the sheep hear his voice, and he calls his own sheep by name and leads them out. When he puts forth all his own, he goes ahead of them, and the sheep follow him because they know his voice.

Do you feel rushed to make a decision right now?
○ yes   ○ no   If so, in what way?

_____

What do God's pre-planned purposes suggest to you
about pressures to rush decisions?

_____

I had a friend who was a financially-struggling seminary student. She wanted to purchase a new car. A pushy salesman pressured her to make a decision. She felt nervous and unsure so she walked away from the offer. Two weeks later an anonymous donor blessed her with a free car.

Wait for the Father to lead you. If you do not feel assurance in a decision, then wait. You will be glad you did.

What has the Holy Spirit taught you as you studied today?

_____

_____

_____

What is God asking you to do as a result of today's study?

_____

_____

Write a prayer responding to God's commands to you.

_____

_____

_____

_____

1. Jan Johnson, *When the Soul Listens* (Colorado Springs: NavPress, 1999), 129.
2. Elisabeth Elliot, *A Slow and Certain Light* (Waco, TX :Wordbooks, 1973), 89.

Day 4 GOD'S CHALLENGING VOICE

HE SPEAKS
The gate is narrow and the way is hard, that leads to life. Matthew 7:14, RSV

I KNOW THE LORD IS SPEAKING *to me when I'm not particularly thrilled with what He is saying.* Forgive him. Be kinder to her. Visit the prisoners. Change your attitude. Submit to authority. Stop controlling things. It's not about you, Ellie—get over yourself! *I love Jesus and have been enjoying a relationship with Him for almost 35 years BUT my stubborn Italian flesh still collides with God's perfect will for my life. How I yearn to arrive at a place when my consistent response to the Lord's voice will be that of Jesus: "Not my will Lord, but yours." —Ellie Lofaro*

God's voice always reveals His character and His purposes. He invites us to cooperate with Him to carry out the plans He prepared before time began. Remaining open to God's plans, however, can be hard for me.

I seek the Lord and prepare a message on what I believe a group of women need to hear. Then I travel with my plans in place. I have learned not to tell anyone what I will be talking about, because very often the Lord impresses on me the need to address an entirely different topic with the women as a conference progresses. Hours or even minutes before I am supposed to give the message, I sense God leading me in another direction based on what He is doing at the event. I always feel scared and uncomfortable when this happens, but God's power and anointing will only rest on His message, not mine. To affect lives with God's power I must go with God's plans.

Have you ever heard the Master say something very difficult to you? If you haven't, I question whether you have ever heard Him say anything at all.[1]
—Oswald Chambers

THE CHALLENGE OF HIS PLAN

When God speaks through His Spirit, His Word, and circumstances, I find that His message challenges me because His purposes are always higher then mine. When followed in obedience, His Word causes me to step away from the comfort zone of my natural abilities and into the realm of His supernatural possibilities.

His word causes me to step away from the comfort zone

of my natural _____ and into the realm

of His supernatural _____.

When God speaks, He frequently asks me to do something I would never do on my own. He reminded Isaiah, "As the heavens are higher than the earth, so are My ways higher than your ways and My thoughts than your thoughts" (Isa. 55:9). When He speaks, His words will challenge us to do something outside of our normal realm of acting and thinking.

Jan Johnson writes, "If what you sense from God never contains anything that surprises you, you're probably making it up yourself. It is likely that God is speaking when what you hear sounds nothing like you, or when it is so simple or so profound you would never have thought of it."[2]

When a thought comes to you out of left field, don't ignore it. Check inward to see if the Holy Spirit is encouraging you to pursue it. I often know God is speaking when a thought occurs to me that makes me feel surprised and maybe even uncomfortable because I know I can't do it in my own power. Then when I take that thought to the Lord and the Holy Spirit brings conviction that will not let me rest until I move forward, I know it is God.

Look at the following examples. How did God's instructions challenge the listener?

Moses (Ex. 3:1-10) _____

Gideon (Judg. 6:12-14) _____

Rich man (Luke 18:18-23) _____

He wants you to see what He can do when you admit you can't.

God's word will challenge you. He wants you to experience His supernatural activity. He wants you to see what He can do when you admit you can't.

In Matthew 4, Satan tried to get the Messiah to cop out on what the Father wanted to accomplish. The voices of our enemy or our egos will always give us the easier option. They never encourage us to tap into divine resources.

On the graph at the top of page 97, list decisions you are in the midst of making now. Describe the easy and difficult options for each. I have given an example of my own.

Situation	Challenging answer	Easy answer
resolving an argument with my husband	keep quiet and take the matter to the Lord	make my opinion heard immediately

How might your decision to choose the more challenging road in the areas you listed make room for God's power to be seen in you? Plan to discuss this with your small group.

_____

_____

We feel tempted to do the opposite of what God asks, because it's easier. But God's voice commands the option that will display His power. He desires to show Himself strong in you and will encourage you to do things that require trust and faith. The Enemy's voice says, "You don't have enough. You are not able. You can't." The voice of the Holy Spirit says, "I have enough. I am able through you. I can!"

When you face two options and each seems to please God, consider the one that displays God's glory, power, and strength. This makes room for God to reveal Himself to you and show Himself through you.

God wants us to see the wondrous things He will accomplish in us. Don't be fearful about the hard road He may ask you to take. Be encouraged and excited about seeing His divine, supernatural activity in and through you.

What has the Holy Spirit taught you as you studied today?

_____

_____

One of the ways we know his voice is that its content is such that he keeps us at a point of trusting him for something new—in ourselves, in our loved ones, in our ministry. Trusting him for deeper levels. For more growth. For wider usage. And always advancing from faith to faith.[3]
—Peter Lord

What is God asking you to do as a result of today's study?

_____

_____

Write a prayer responding to God's commands to you.

_____

_____

_____

---

1. Oswald Chambers, *My Utmost for His Highest: Special Updated Edition* (Grand Rapids: Discovery House Publications, 1995), August 17.
2. Jan Johnson, *When the Soul Listens* (Colorado Springs: NavPress, 1999), 112.
3. Peter Lord, *Hearing God* (Grand Rapids: Baker Book House, 2005), 138.

GOD'S INTERCONNECTED VOICE

Day 5

HE SPEAKS
Let's see how inventive we can be in encouraging love and helping out, not avoiding worshiping together as some do but spurring each other on, especially as we see the big Day approaching.
Hebrews 10:24-25,
THE MESSAGE

I KNOW THE LORD IS SPEAKING *to me when He confirms things to me through His Word that are already happening around me. There have been many times that I've allowed anxious thoughts to consume me and cause me to be confused and downcast. I have found, though, when I've taken the time to open His Word for help He will speak very specifically to that hurt or stress and cause it to flee. Lately God has also used dear friends and the church community around me to speak into my life in a very powerful way and to confirm again what I felt He was saying. When I'm hearing the same theme from a few different sources around me I know that I need to posture my heart to hear Him and not miss where He's leading.—Christy Nockels*

The church is the family of God and a mechanism through which He speaks to His children. No Christian can accomplish God's complete purpose without being a member of a local church. You were not born again into a family without siblings. The church is God's family, set apart to accomplish His purposes. Although the church is not needed for Christians to have direct access to God, it is a very necessary part of hearing, understanding, and participating in the will of God. Every member of the church has been specifically placed and gifted to accomplish those purposes in the world. You are not a believer and a part of the family of God in this generation by chance. God allowed you to be a part of a local group of believers so He can accomplish His tasks on earth.

Many Christians have become comfortable just watching TV evangelists or listening to their favorite preacher on the radio. This creates a complete lack of participation for the believer. You do not have to assist in accomplishing the purposes of God while curled up on your couch watching or listening. These activities are a blessing to the body of Christ but should never take the place of being involved and connected with your brothers and sisters.

Hebrews 10:24-25
Let us consider how to stimulate one another to love and good deeds, not forsaking our own assembling together, as is the habit of some, but encouraging one another; and all the more as you see the day drawing near.

THE BODY

The church is the body of Christ (see 1 Cor. 12:27). We have been purposefully positioned in the body to help carry out the necessary functions that will bring God glory. To accomplish the plans of God, the individual members of the body must cooperate by actively participating in their area of gifting within the body. When we do this we are fulfilling our function individually and collectively.

Paul sought to illustrate this principal to the members of the church at Corinth. Read his explanation in 1 Corinthians 12:21 and write your paraphrase of the verse in the margin.

Jerry Jr. is my youngest son. When he was still crawling, he got comfortable using his hands and feet to get around. He became frustrated when his hands were not free to do other things. I would encourage him to pick his hands up off the floor and use them for other purposes, but he persisted in using his hands as his tools to get around. It wasn't until he figured out his feet were for walking and his hands for picking things up that he really began to enjoy living.

Frustration occurs in any body when one part doesn't want to do what it is supposed to. Within the church, when we try to be or do something that is not what we were created for, we not only cause frustration but we also keep the body from reaching its full potential to accomplish God's purposes. Any part of the physical body that becomes detached from the body will no longer flourish and experience the protection that comes from being connected. Without the body, you can't do what you were created to do.

Without the body, you can't do what you were created to do.

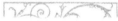

Are you a member of a local church? ○ yes ○ no
Why or why not?

_____

What gifts has the Lord given you to encourage and edify the church to accomplish His purposes in and through them?

_____

THE VOICE OF GOD IN THE CHURCH

God can and will use the church to help acquaint you with His leading in your life. He can and will speak to you and direct you to His will using the members of the local body of Christ.

 God can and will _____ to me and _____

me to His will using the members of _____.

The speaking ministry the Lord has entrusted to me really began when, as a young girl, I responded to a need in my local church. My parents had a flannel board with paper characters to tell Bible stories. My mom used this to share God's Word with us. I would often take the board to my room to teach my imaginary class.

Our children's ministry has always been a thriving ministry to the young people in our congregation. My aunt Elizabeth has been the children's ministry leader there for 25 years. When I was about 12 years old she asked me to lead the children in a Sunday School lesson. I spent long hours trying to figure out how I could tell the story in a way that would be appealing to them.

After that my aunt sensed that I needed to be a regular part of what God was doing in that ministry. Although I didn't realize it at the time, this was God's way of speaking to me through my church. The body was in need. He gifted me to accomplish the task and gave me a willing heart.

God speaks through the church. When God allows you to see a need in your local church that tugs at your heart or continues to be a recurring thought, don't be afraid to take this to God for further direction. If God is speaking to you through the church to accomplish His plans, you will notice a pattern in your Bible study, prayer, and circumstances that points you in the same direction.

What needs do you currently see in your church?

_____

Which of these needs tug at your heart?

_____

God's plan will often require you to step away from the comfort zone of your natural abilities so you can experience His supernatural possibilities. You may see a need in the body and feel encouraged by the Holy Spirit to do something you do not feel equipped to do. If God calls you, He will equip you. Give Him the opportunity to display His supernatural activity as He uses you for His glory.

> If God calls you, He will equip you.

While Henry Blackaby was in seminary, his church had a need. He was asked to be the music and education director. He didn't feel equipped since he had never sung in a choir nor led music. He felt God was leading him to respond despite his inexperience, so he willingly obeyed. He served in this capacity for two years, and then the church voted him to be their pastor! He hadn't preached many sermons; but God equipped him, and now he has blessed millions of people.[1]

What might God be able to do in and through us as we connect with our family in Christ?

What has the Holy Spirit taught you as you studied today?

_____

_____

What is God asking you to do as a result of today's study?

_____

_____

Write a prayer responding to God's commands to you.

_____

_____

_____

_____

---

1. Henry Blackaby and Claude V. King, *Experiencing God: Knowing and Doing the Will of God* (Nashville: Lifeway Press, 2004), 106.

∽THIS WEEK AT A GLANCE∽

Write the key principles from this week's study:

Day 1: _____

_____

Day 2: _____

_____

Day 3: _____

_____

Day 4: _____

_____

Day 5: _____

_____

Look back at your notes from the end of each day of study. List three things the Holy Spirit has encouraged you to do as a result of this week's study.

1. _____

2. _____

3. _____

What immediate steps will you take to respond in obedience?

_____

_____

_____

_____

RESPONDING TO GOD'S VOICE

*Naaman was furious and went away and said, "Behold, I thought,
'He will surely come out to me and stand and call on the name of the LORD his God,
and wave his hand over the place and cure the leper.'"*
2 Kings 5:11

When God speaks, your response is to _____, not to _____.

Three Preconceived Expectations that Hinder God's Healing

1. the means of _____

2. the method of _____

3. the means of _____

Communication: _____ _____ from us the opportunity to
hear God's voice.

Ministry: _____ _____ from us the opportunity to hear
God's voice.

Deliverance: plain and simple—_____.

Responding to God's Voice

Day 1   THE ONLY APPROPRIATE RESPONSE

HE SPEAKS
His mother said to the servants, "Whatever He says to you, do it."
John 2:5

I KNOW WHEN THE LORD IS *speaking to me because literally the air around me changes. There is a stillness that settles all my raging emotions and questions and simply bids me to be silent, listen, and consider what I hear. And then it's almost as if it comes from the center of my being—the answer, the revelation, the instruction and it is sealed in this definite place inside of me that I can't describe. I only know that I must do what I've been prompted to do. If I resist I can't breathe, but when I say yes and obey the most incredible sense of knowing and peace overtakes me and the matter is settled once and for all.* —Michelle McKinney Hammond

Matthew 5:8
Blessed are the pure in heart, for they shall see God.

As I was seeking to hear God's voice more clearly, God allowed me to cross paths with Mary Elaine Cline. Her godly lifestyle and experience with God whet the appetite of all who meet her. Mary Elaine's life is a testament to the power of God.

Recently we talked about why some believers experience the power of God more often than others. Her response was one I will never forget. She said, "I think I see God's supernatural activity so clearly in my life because I have decided that the only appropriate response to Him is complete obedience. I am committed to obeying His leading no matter how absurd His instructions may be." This kind of response lays the groundwork for God to do incredible things in her life.

How you choose to respond to God is more important than hearing from Him. He doesn't just speak to be heard. He speaks to be obeyed.

Time and time again, God demonstrated His ability in and through Abraham because Abraham was willing to obey whatever God told him. Abraham was called "the friend of God" (Jas. 2:23) not because he heard God's voice but because he was committed to obeying God's voice.

> Abraham was called "the friend of God" not because he heard God's voice but because he was committed to obeying God's voice.

🌼 **God doesn't just speak to be** _____.

He speaks to be _____.

WHATEVER HE SAYS TO YOU DO IT

In the first week of our study together, we talked about how we should plan to obey God. Sister, we have come full circle. Obedience is not only the key that keeps the door of communication open between you and God but the only appropriate response when He speaks.

One of Abraham's most unbelievable acts of obedience came when he was given these very shocking instructions by God: "Take now your son, your only son, whom you love, Isaac, and go to the land of Moriah, and offer him there as a burnt offering" (Gen. 22:2).

God had promised Abraham a great nation from his offspring. God was asking something that not only sounded unreasonable but seemed to contradict His own word.

Has God ever asked you to do something that seemed shocking and unreasonable? ○ yes ○ no If so, what was your response? Plan to share your experience with your small group.

_____

> The worse thing you can do— the quickest way to become insensitive— is to ignore an impression. So you must commit yourself to listening to your Lord for the purpose of responding to what he says, and you must not allow yourself to hear without responding.[1]
> —Peter Lord

Recently I addressed some women at a retreat in California. During the event, a woman shared her testimony about how God is using her to minister to children in Jamaica. As she spoke, I immediately sensed the Lord telling me to bless her with a very specific financial gift. The impression resonated with such authority I had no doubt God was speaking. I wish I could say I immediately gave without question, but I debated with God for awhile. The amount I felt He was leading me to give was large. Jerry and I were in the midst of a huge financial transition in our own lives, and to give away that amount of money to someone else at a time like this seemed ridiculous.

When the thought persisted and my Spirit-led conscience brought conviction, I gave the money even though it didn't make good financial sense. Within days, I saw evidence of God's favor on my decision to obey.

God's response to my obedience was so abundant that I immediately began to regret the many times I considered God's way too difficult and chose another option. How many times have I forfeited God's blessing in my life? I want to see God's supernatural activity. I don't just want to hear about it and watch it from afar. I want to experience it. As Abraham's difficult obedience yielded supernatural results, so will ours. Over and over Scripture makes clear that the determining factor for experiencing God is obedience. We must learn to make obedience a habit regardless of our feelings. Like my friend Mary Elaine and the patriarch Abraham, our motto should be, "Whatever He says to you, do it."

If you are ready to make this motto your own, write it in the margin.
Sign and date it as a reminder of when you made this commitment.
If you don't feel you can honestly make the commitment now, wait
until later. But take time to ask the Lord what is holding you back.

The hardest part of listening to God's voice is obeying. From the beginning of the Old Testament to the end of the New, Scripture continually stresses obedience.

Look up the follow verses. What do they say about obeying God?

Exodus 15:26-27: _____

Exodus 23:22: _____

Deuteronomy 31:12: _____

Luke 8:18: _____

John 14:15: _____

God knows what is best and only requires us to obey so that we may experience it. He desires to bless us with His most special gifts, and we experience them when we commit to the only appropriate response: complete and immediate obedience.

What has the Holy Spirit taught you as you studied today?

_____

_____

What is God asking you to do as a result of today's study?

_____

_____

Write a prayer responding to God's commands to you.

_____

_____

_____

---

1. Peter Lord, *Hearing God* (Grand Rapids: Baker Book House, 1988), 39.

Day 2 THE ONLY APPROPRIATE RESPONSE (PART 2)

TWO IMPORTANT PREREQUISITES *to hearing God clearly are to have an open vertical relationship with the Lord and to be submitted to His plan for our lives. If there is unconfessed sin or continued disobedience in our lives, there will be a "closed heaven" above us and a disruption in hearing from the Lord. God cannot draw near to us while we are walking away from Him through disobedience at the same time. —Jim Cymbala*

HE SPEAKS

He who has My commandments and keeps them is the one who loves Me; and he who loves Me will be loved by My Father, and I will love him and will disclose Myself to him. John 14:21

It was a bright Texas morning. I sat in my office, more commonly known as the kitchen table, with an open Bible before me. That day my prayer time consisted of only one request: "Lord, reveal yourself to me. I want to see you move in the practical circumstances of my life." When my prayer time ended, my eyes fell on John 14:21: "The person who has My commands and keeps them is the one who [really] loves me; ... and I ... will show (reveal, manifest) Myself to him. [I will let Myself be clearly seen by him and make Myself real to him]" (AMP).

With these words, the Holy Spirit challenged me, "Priscilla, you want to see me? Get busy being radically obedient to me."

The definition of the original Greek word used for *reveal* in John 14:21 means "to exhibit, to appear in person and to declare." Everyone who is a believer is privileged to know the love of God. However, an invasion of His manifest presence in the life of a believer and a deeper revelation of the person of God will come to those who choose obedience as the habit of their lives.

❧ THE PRICE OF OBEDIENCE ❧

Our willingness to obey depends on whether we think the cost outweighs the benefits. We will discuss some of these costs in tomorrow's lesson. We need to recognize them to respond appropriately to God's word. We will usually refuse to follow God's direction when we think what we have to give up is greater than what we will gain. As a result, we miss God's blessing, experience His judgment, and break the intimacy that allows our spiritual ears to hear what He has to say to us in the future.

Obedience will always produce benefits that far outweigh the consequences of disobedience.

Obedience will always produce benefits that outweigh the consequences of disobedience. In the short run it may appear our way is best, but we will soon see that obedience would have given us access to His supernatural power.

In what way is it difficult for you to believe God's benefits outweigh the cost of obedience?

_____

_____

Read 2 Chronicles 20:17-24 and John 2:1-11. For each story, answer the following questions.

What did God ask them to do?

2 Chronicles 20:17-24_____

John 2:1-11 _____

What did it cost to respond in obedience to God?

2 Chronicles 20:17-24_____

John 2:1-11 _____

What was their reward for obeying?

2 Chronicles 20:17-24 _____

John 2:1-11 _____

What would have been different if they had chosen not to obey?

2 Chronicles 20:17-24 _____

John 2:1-11 _____

THE REWARDS OF OBEDIENCE

When you choose to obey, you will find God rewards you with His power, presence, and supernatural blessing. When Abraham obeyed God, he experienced a blessing beyond his dreams. I believe a correlation exists between the cost of Abraham's obedience and the magnificent blessing that resulted. The higher the price you pay to obey God, the greater the reward you can expect from Him.

When I choose to _____ His leading, He will

reward me with His _____, _____,

and _____ blessing.

Read Genesis 22:16-18 in the margin. Underline the rewards Abraham would have missed if he had refused to obey.

Genesis 22:16-18, NLT
This is what the LORD says: Because you have obeyed me and have not withheld even your beloved son, I swear by my own self that I will bless you richly. I will multiply your descendants into countless millions, like the stars of the sky and the sand on the seashore. They will conquer their enemies, and through your descendants, all the nations of the earth will be blessed—all because you have obeyed me.

One of my favorite game shows was "Let's Make A Deal." It offered the contestant a choice between two doors. Behind each one was a present. One would be something great, like a car or trip, while the other was a booby prize. Contestants would debate about which door while being completely in the dark regarding what was behind the doors. Inevitably some contestants would make a choice that they would regret. The prize wouldn't be what they wanted.

You too face two doors. One is marked "obedience," the other says "disobedience." You choose, but He has listed for you what you will find behind each door. It may cost us something to obey, but choosing that door will reap benefits.

What has the Holy Spirit taught you as you studied today?

_____

_____

What is God asking you to do as a result of today's study?

_____

_____

_____

Write a prayer responding to God's commands to you.

_____

_____

_____

_____

Day 3 THE COSTLY RESPONSE

HE SPEAKS

If any of you wants to be my follower … you must put aside your selfish ambition, shoulder your cross, and follow me. If you try to keep your life for yourself, you will lose it. But if you give up

I looked into my friend's frustrated face. I knew she had a heart to hear and obey God, but obedience had been costly. Kimberly was always the ambitious type. As a young child she had grand ideas of what her career and family life would be like. It included a faithful climb up the corporate ladder ending in an appointment as CEO, one husband, two well-adjusted children, and retirement at an early age. She looked forward to spending her later years traveling the world with her spouse.

Although many great things happened in Kimberly's life, many things turned out quite differently from her plan. After college she married her best friend and started her career; but before she could get to a comfortable place of success she got pregnant with twins. One of them had health concerns that required too much attention for her to maintain her fast-paced job. She had to redirect her plans to stay home with her children. Within two years another baby was on the way.

Kimberly found joy in raising her children but often felt she was missing something better. As her children grew and needed less attention, she looked forward to more freedom and possibly returning to the workforce. But as her parents got older their health failed. She knew God was asking her to serve her family and her parents during this season. Her days are now filled with doctor visits, senior citizen activities, and providing for her aging parents. No career success, no traveling, no retirement at an early age. Kimberly is frustrated and tired.

your life for my sake and for the sake of the Good News, you will find true life.
Mark 8:34-35, NLT

Although the circumstance of our lives may be different from Kimberly's, the sentiments of our hearts are often the same. As we seek to discern God's voice and respond appropriately, we can become frustrated because it seems God is steering us away from our cherished goals. Kimberly experienced extra frustration because although she had made a firm decision to hear God's voice and obey, she hadn't truly considered what major adjustments this surrender might entail. She certainly *desired* to hear and obey, but she hadn't counted the cost obedience might require. A life of obedience calls us to prepare for the adjustments God requires. If we don't prepare to modify our plans, we will end up more frustrated and overwhelmed.

 A life of obedience calls me to prepare for the _____ God requires.

Nicodemus had to modify his belief system to be saved (John 3). The woman at the well modified her actions and became an evangelist to her whole city (John 4). Joshua had to forgo his battle plans to experience victory at Jericho (Josh. 6) and Gideon had to relinquish his ideas of what a good, strong army looked like before going into battle (Judg. 6). We all have to adjust to appropriately respond to God.

As you have gone through this study, God has spoken to you. What modifications have you been asked to make in your:

beliefs: _____

traditions: _____

plans: _____

relationships: _____

other: _____

In Matthew 11:28, Jesus offered an invitation to a group of His followers. He said, "Come to Me, all who are weary and heavy-laden, and I will give you rest." With these words He invited them to join the kingdom of God, but with one stipulation: they had to receive what Jesus offered, abandoning their beliefs about religion, traditions concerning worship, and plans of how they would receive the Messiah. They had to relinquish their preconceived notions to experience the rest of Jesus.

SURRENDER

Proverbs 19:21
Many are the plans
in a man's heart,
But the counsel
of the LORD, it
will stand.

Deciding to adjust our lives in obedience to God requires surrender. Proverbs 19:21 reveals that only God's purposes will prevail. Any plan we devise on our own will not reap eternal dividends. If we want to see God operating in our lives, we must adopt His plans and accept His invitation to be part of them.

Please don't misunderstand. Don't let the Enemy discourage you into thinking you will never see your dreams become reality.

> Look back on page 109 and read the key principle for that day.
> Describe how the principle dispels this lie of the Enemy.

_____

The Holy Spirit is at work in you to change your desires to match up with the Father's desires. We must keep our life plans *flexible*. Never make concrete plans without leaving room for God to do something different.

> Choose one of the following characters and record what adjustments
> they make to follow God's leading.
>   Abraham (Gen. 17:6-7,17)   Moses (Ex. 3:1-10)
>   Hosea (Hos. 1:2; 3:1)   Jesus (Matt. 26:39)
>   disciples (Luke 14:33)

_____

_____

> In the margin, list adjustments you would have to make for your
> plans to align with God's plans right now. Put a plus sign beside the
> ones you are willing to make and a minus sign beside those you are
> hesitant to make.

> Talk honestly with the Lord about those with a minus sign. Ask
> Him to give you the courage to surrender so you can experience
> His best for you.

Complete obedience to God requires a commitment to modify and change our plans at a moment's notice. Will you make a decision today to surrender to the Lord completely?

What has the Holy Spirit taught you as you studied today?

_____

_____

What is God asking you to do as a result of today's study?

_____

_____

Write a prayer responding to God's commands to you.

_____

_____

_____

Day 4 THE IMMEDIATE RESPONSE

I KNOW GOD IS SPEAKING *to me when I am awakened during the night and it's difficult to get back to sleep. I try not to second guess my sudden state of awakening … whether I was nudged by God or something I ate before bed. I just lie there and talk to God. I talk openly and honestly to Him. I tell Him how much I love Him. If I have anything that concerns me, I present my requests to Him. I know He is ready to set my mind at ease so I talk to Him about anything that weighs on my heart and mind. I have the assurance that no matter what time of day or night, God is as close to me as my prayers.* —Babbie Mason

HE SPEAKS
Today, if you would hear His voice Do not harden your hearts.
Psalm 95:7-8

For two years I dated a young godly man, and I was in love. Our initial months of courtship were wonderful and long overdue. We had been friends for several years before our dating relationship began, and I always had a secret crush on him. Now the feelings were reciprocal and we were having discussions of moving toward marriage. I was thrilled and excited. When we graduated from college and began seminary together, things in our relationship began to change. He seemed to be pulling away, and I sensed the Holy Spirit trying to lead me in another direction as well. Neither of us wanted to follow His directive. We both continued in the relationship for another emotionally tumultuous year knowing the Spirit of God had other plans. Finally, he stopped fighting the Lord and told me it was time to call it quits. I was devastated. I had been holding tightly to this relationship. I was hoping it would end in marriage, and now it was over. I finally did something I should have done long before. I asked God's forgiveness for rebelling against Him, and I surrendered.

Several days later I got a phone call that resulted in me meeting the man who would become my husband. When we got to know each other, we discovered we had attended the same church for over six years. The news that we had been so close for many years saddened me. My delayed response to God's leading had cost me years of emotional heartache and a broken heart, while God's best for me was just a few pews away. I should have been committed to an immediate response to God's leading. God speaks with perfect timing. Our response should be immediate obedience.

Genesis 22:2-3
He said, "Take now your son, your only son, whom you love, Isaac, and go to the land of Moriah, and offer him there as a burnt offering on one of the mountains of which I will tell you." So Abraham rose early in the morning and saddled his donkey, and took two of his young men with him and Isaac his son; and he split wood for the burnt offering, and arose and went to the place of which God had told him.

God speaks with perfect _____. My response should

be _____ obedience.

Abraham knew the blessing in responding to God without delay. When God told him to leave his homeland with no further information on where he was to go, he obeyed immediately with nothing more than God's word for security (Heb. 11:8). On another occasion God instructed him to circumcise every male in his household, and Abraham did it the very same day (Gen. 17:11-14,23). Although he wasn't perfect, Abraham learned the importance of doing what God asked without delay, and he experienced the rewards.

Look carefully at Genesis 22:2-3 in the margin.

How quickly did Abraham respond? _____

How might your response have been different from Abraham's?

_____

Abraham didn't wait for a couple days or weeks to make sure God was sure about what He wanted him to do. Rather, Abraham received instructions and obeyed the next morning. He gave instant, unquestioning obedience despite unbelievably difficult instructions. When the Lord gives me instructions I don't particularly like or am afraid to carry out, the last thing I want to do is get up early in the morning to do it. I often find myself thinking about it, praying over it, talking to friends about it, or even trying to ignore it. The Holy Spirit has instructed me to leave many movies, put down many books, desert many conversations, and turn off many television shows. More often than not, my obedience is not as quick as it should be. What about you?

Psalm 119:60, NLT
I will hurry, without lingering, to obey your commands.

Has the Lord given you instructions this week to which you have taken too much time to respond? If so, what were they?

_____

What was the reason for your delay?

_____

Jeremiah 7:23, NLT
Obey me, and I will be your God, and you will be my people. Only do as I say and all will be well.

THE CONSEQUENCES OF DELAY

As a result of my unwillingness to immediately obey God in my dating relationship, I carried around emotional baggage that affected my marriage in its early stages. Had I obeyed without question, I would have saved myself and my future husband a lot of turmoil. God knows your life from beginning to end. He knows all the details necessary to take you from where you are to where He wants you to be and keep you in His perfect will.

Moses experienced the consequences of delayed obedience. God wanted him to tell Pharaoh to release the Hebrew people from captivity. This task seemed impossible. Moses had a long discussion with God as to why he could not do what God asked. As a result, he was limited in his ability to serve the people of God.

Isaiah 50:4, NLT
The Sovereign LORD has given me his words of wisdom ... Morning by morning he wakens me and opens my understanding to his will.

Read the following examples of people who did not respond immediately to God. How do these stories mirror your own?

Luke 1:5-25 _____

_____

Acts 4:32; 5:1-10 _____

_____

YES LORD

Would that ram have been caught in the bush if Abraham had delayed his obedience?

The only appropriate answer when we hear God speaking is "Yes, Lord!" Abraham immediately obeyed God and he received divine intervention. I've always wondered—would that ram have been caught in the bush if Abraham had delayed his obedience? God alone knows if that ram would have been available for Abraham to sacrifice if he had waited to do what God told him. Immediate obedience caused Abraham to intersect with God's deliverance on that mountaintop.

Several years ago I intended to go back to graduate school for my doctoral degree. The prospect of being back in school thrilled me. I went through all the necessary arrangements to retrieve an admissions application. I spent many hours making sure everything was filled out accurately before packaging it all up and driving to the school to drop it off. I'll never forget the excitement I felt knowing I would soon be back in school.

On the drive to the seminary to drop off my application the Holy Spirit spoke clearly to my heart. He said, *I didn't tell you I wanted you back in school. You want to be back in school, but I have other plans.* This immediate impression was so strong I knew God was speaking to me. I thought about going ahead to drop off the application and then talking it over with my husband after I got home, but I was reminded about the principle of immediate obedience. I took the next exit and went home.

That was four years ago. In all these years I have never once had a desire to go back to school for that degree. God completely removed the desire and replaced it with other things. I am amazed and humbled by all God has done. I didn't know at the time all God had planned for me, but He did; and my immediate obedience has paid off.

What might the Lord accomplish in and through you if you responded immediately to what He asks you to do?

What has the Holy Spirit taught you as you studied today?

_____

_____

What is God asking you to do as a result of today's study?

_____

_____

_____

Write a prayer responding to God's commands to you.

_____

_____

_____

_____

_____

Day 5 THE COMMITTED RESPONSE

Our spiritual ear will never be sensitive to his voice if we have a personal agenda to which we are already committed. God leads and speaks to the humble who have surrendered their plans and want to do His will. With an "open heaven" and a surrendered will, we will be able to clearly hear God's voice in our hearts. —Jim Cymbala

HE SPEAKS

The Sovereign LORD has spoken to me, and I have listened. I do not rebel or turn away. … Therefore, I have set my face like a stone, determined to do his will. And I know that I will triumph. Isaiah 50:5,7, NLT

Hernando Cortes was the Spanish conqueror of Mexico. In 1518 he convinced Diego Velazquez, governor of Cuba, to give him command of an expedition to this new land to establish a colony and capture its treasures. He was given 11 ships and 600 men to make the journey. By March of 1519, after months of travel and hardship, they arrived at their destination. He knew his men were tired and wanted to return home. To prevent thoughts of retreat, he burned the ships. Hernando Cortes was committed to the task at hand. He was so dedicated that he annihilated all options for escape.

Often I am willing to obey God but I want to keep my ships up and working just in case. It is comforting to have a plan B waiting when obedience isn't convenient anymore. But God desires that we "burn our ships," annihilate any other means of departure, and throw ourselves wholeheartedly into what He has asked of us. This requires radical faith and radical trust in God.

This week we have learned that God doesn't speak simply to be heard; He speaks to be obeyed. To respond to God in the way He deserves, we must be committed to obedience to God.

 To respond to God in the way He _____,

I must be _____ to obedience to God.

❧ THE EXAMPLE OF ABRAHAM ❧

Despite the unbelievably difficult instructions God gave Abraham, he not only obeyed immediately but he also obeyed with commitment.

Look at Genesis 22:3 and make a list of all Abraham took with him to Mt. Moriah to make the sacrifice to the Lord.

_____

Considering why Abraham was going to the mountain, what seems to be missing from the list?

_____

Abraham took no lamb or other animal to sacrifice at the last minute and rescue him from his dilemma. Abraham didn't take a plan B. Surely those were the longest 50 miles he ever traveled. During this 72-hour trip he had plenty of time to change his mind. In spite of the apparent loss of his son's life, he was so committed to the Lord that he knew God's plan and his obedience to that plan were more important and rewarding than if he followed his own.

On page 111 you listed some modifications the Lord has been asking you to make during this study. Name one of those things:

_____

Are you committed to obedience in this area or do you have a plan B?
◯ I'm committed.   ◯ I have a plan B.
If you have a plan B, what is it?

_____

_____

What "ships" is the Lord asking you to burn so you can move forward in committed obedience to Him?

_____

Scripture has a name for believers who desire to hear from God but have a plan B waiting in the wings: double-minded (see Jas. 1:7-8 in margin). James says if we are double-minded, we should expect to receive nothing from the Lord. The Lord knows our hearts. He is completely aware of whether or not we have fully decided to obey Him no matter what His instructions. If He sees in us a heart not single-mindedly given to obedience, He may choose not to reveal His Word. If you are not hearing from God, ask the Lord if double-mindedness is the cause.

James 1:7-8
Let not that man expect that he will receive anything from the Lord, being a double-minded man, unstable in all his ways.

Committed obedience can be frightening unless we know God is good and kind. He has our best interest in mind and has a plan for us that is for our good (see Jer. 29:11). When you give yourself wholly to Him, you can be sure He will give you His strength to accomplish the mission of obedience.

COMMITTED TO THE GRAVE

Hemet, California was once known for gang activity and drug business. The gang activity was so widespread that it wasn't uncommon to see three generations of one family with membership in the most pervasive group, the First Street Gang. The violence was so rampant that even police officers wouldn't go into the area without back up. Nine methamphetamine labs supplied more than a million people a year. The dominant religion was Scientology and a meditation center stood as the centerpiece of the town, a symbol of the New Age fetish. A spirit of competition, particularly among the pastors, marked the Christian community. Known as a pastor's graveyard, Hemet was the last place most pastors wanted to be in ministry.

God called the Beckets to this valley, but they didn't want to be there. When they arrived, they didn't even unpack their bags, hoping God would let them leave. But they were soon assured this was God's calling on their lives. To show their commitment to God's word, the Beckets bought a cemetery plot as a way of saying, "There's no way out. Unless God tells us differently, we will die here."

In the years since their commitment to God's leading and with the help of other area pastors, Hemet has completely changed. Cult membership has sunk to less than .003 percent of the population. First Street Gang members have gotten saved and disbanded the group. The drug trade has dropped by 75 percent. Even the New Age Meditation Center was demolished by a fire that didn't destroy anything else. Government officials, officers, and teachers have gotten saved. Hemet schools used to be the laughing stock of California and now have the highest scores and lowest drop-out rates. Churches and pastors aren't competing anymore, they are coming together to build the kingdom of God. All because of an unrelenting commitment to obedience.

What has the Holy Spirit taught you as you studied today?

_____

_____

_____

What is God asking you to do as a result of today's study?

_____

_____

_____

Write a prayer responding to God's commands to you.

_____

_____

_____

_____

_____

_____

∽◯ THIS WEEK AT A GLANCE ◯∾

Write the key principles from this week's study:

Day 1: _____

_____

Day 2: _____

_____

Day 3: _____

_____

Day 4: _____

_____

Day 5: _____

_____

Look back at your notes from the end of each day of study. List three things the Holy Spirit has encouraged you to do as a result of this week's study.

1. _____

2. _____

3. _____

What immediate steps will you take to respond in obedience?

_____

_____

_____

_____

Leader Guide

This guide will help you set up and lead your group. You will be reviewing with participants the material they studied through the week. As you come to know your group, you will better discern which questions to discuss each week.

OVERVIEW AND COURSE DESIGN

This guide provides directions for leading a seven-session group study. A leader kit is also available (001315095), containing DVDs with Priscilla's video messages to be used during the group sessions. While the video messages are valuable to the study, you may do the study using only the member book. Choose activities that will best meet the needs of your group.

Sessions require a minimum of one hour. To allow adequate discussion time, 90 minutes would be preferable. Some groups may choose a more flexible schedule such as viewing and discussing the video one week and discussing the print study the next. Pray and follow the Holy Spirit's leadership in your schedule. Note the varying video session lengths on the DVDs.

On DVD 2 you will find a bonus segment containing a roundtable discussion with Priscilla and several of her friends. This segment is approximately 30 minutes long and can be used any time you choose. You may want to use it during session 7 because of the short length of the video session.

If your group is too large for effective group discussion, watch the video as a large group and discuss in smaller groups.

BEGINNING A BIBLE STUDY GROUP

- Pray for God's leadership; ask for His help in all arrangements, including bringing to the study those people who have a hunger to hear His voice and a willingness to obey.
- Reserve your meeting place and time. Arrange for childcare if needed.
- Promote the study in your church and community. The leader kit contains promotional video segments that can be used for in-church promotion as well as broadcast on local television. You may choose to offer an opportunity for women to preregister for the study to get a preliminary count. Have member books available for participants at the first small-group session.
- Arrange to have a DVD player in your meeting room each week.
- Enlist the number of group facilitators you need for the number of groups you anticipate.

RESPONSIBILITIES OF FACILITATORS

Prayer

Pray for your group as a whole; for individual members; for your leadership of the group; and that members will look forward to hearing and obeying God.

Time and Preparation

Honor participants' time by beginning and ending on time. Be prepared to facilitate the group. Complete each week's assignments. You do not have to have all the answers, but you need to be familiar with the material.

Safe Discussion Group

Establish a safe learning and sharing environment where no one is intimidated and no one dominates the group.

Lead the Sessions

Let the group know you will facilitate the session—not lecture—and that you don't know everything about discerning God's voice. You will guide the group as you help each other learn about the material they studied during the week.

❈ SESSION ONE ❈
Anticipating the Voice of God

Before the Session

1. Make a name tag for yourself. Provide markers and name tags for participants. Have paper and pens or pencils available for use during the session.
2. Preview video session 1.
3. Look through the entire book to familiarize yourself with the content and Bible-study method. Review the "About the Study" and "Introduction" sections and be ready to explain to participants what they can expect from the study.
4. Have copies of the member book available.

During the Session

1. Have participants introduce themselves using an adjective that describes their personality. Introduce yourself first to break the ice and give group members an example to follow. The goal is to begin learning names and personalities.

2. Welcome members to the study. Pay particular attention to newcomers from the community or church. Thank participants for their attendance and their creative personality adjectives. Explain that this session will overview the content, explain the learning approach, and allow members to get acquainted. Lead in an opening prayer for the group and for attentive hearts to discern God's voice.
3. Overview the course. Explain that application is very important to this study. Their individual, daily study will begin the process of application and the small-group discussion will continue the process. Share with the group that together you will discuss concepts you studied during the week, flesh out the concepts, and begin to apply them to your lives. Stress confidentiality of things shared in the small group.
4. Provide participants with a sheet of paper and pen or pencil if needed. Explain that you are about to take a pop quiz. Ask them to number their papers from 1-7. Allow time for group members to respond to each question.
   1. Who does God talk to?
   2. Does God talk to you?
   3. How do you know God talks to you?
   4. When does God talk to you?
   5. How does God talk to you?
   6. Why does God talk to you?
   7. What do you want to get from this study?

   The purpose of this exercise is to help participants realize some of what they know about discerning God's voice and how they know it.
5. Direct participants to complete the viewer guide on page 7 as they watch video session 1 [34:45].
6. Close with prayer for diligent reading, studying, and thinking about hearing God's voice.

SESSION TWO
The Holy Spirit

Before the Session

1. Provide markers and name tags. Be sure to wear your name tag as members arrive.
2. Study week 1 and complete the learning activities. Make your own list of questions to ask during the group session. See the suggested list under During the Session. Give special attention to activities that tell participants they will discuss them in their group session.
3. Preview video session 2.

During the Session

1. Greet participants as they arrive. Open with prayer.
2. Direct members to their member books. Refer to your list of questions to discuss as a group; share the page number as you ask each question so members can refer back to their responses. Possible questions include:
   a. What attributes of God did you identify in Habakkuk 1:12-13? (p. 10)
   b. What result have you experienced from acting before God spoke? (p. 12)
   c. How do you usually respond to God's word even when it may be something you do not want to hear? (p. 16)
   d. How can you turn everyday tasks into opportunities to listen for God? (p. 19)
   e. What visual stimuli distract you from turning to God? (p. 20)
   f. How does our faith or lack of it impact our journey regardless of God's actions? (see p. 25)
3. Direct participants to complete the viewer guide on page 27 as they watch video session 2 [47:05].
4. Close in prayer for anticipation to hear God's voice.

SESSION THREE
The Voice of the Holy Spirit

Before the Session

1. Provide markers and name tags.
2. Study week 2 and complete the learning activities. Mark questions to ask during the group session. Give special attention to activities that tell participants they will discuss them in their group session.
3. Preview video session 3.

During the Session

1. Greet participants as they arrive. Open with prayer.
2. Direct members to their member books. Refer to your list of questions to discuss as a group; share the page number as you ask each question so members can refer back to their responses. Possible questions include:
   a. Why is God's Spirit better than His speaking through sensational means? (p. 30)
   b. How have your actions and attitudes changed since the Spirit resides in you? (p. 33)
   c. Review and discuss the five Ms. (p. 33)
   d. In what areas do you struggle with the battle between flesh and spirit? (p. 38)
   e. How would you describe the difference between seeking God's will and seeking Him? (p. 42)
3. Direct participants to complete the viewer guide on page 45 as they watch video session 3 [36:36].
4. Close in prayer for identifying the Spirit's voice.

❈ SESSION FOUR ❈
God's Voice Reveals His Character

Before the Session
1. Study week 3 and complete the learning activities. As you study, list questions to ask during the group session. Give special attention to activities that tell participants they will discuss them in their group session.
2. Preview video session 4.

During the Session
1. Greet participants as they arrive. Encourage perseverance for the remainder of the course. Open with prayer.
2. Refer to your list of questions to discuss as a group; share the page number as you ask each question so members can refer back to their responses. Possible questions include:
   a. How has God used multiple means to confirm what He was saying to you? (p. 48)
   b. In what ways do we hold each other in bondage to our convictions? (p. 51)
   c. Discuss the true/false statements on page 52.
   d. What kind of person did Paul have in mind when he advised us to be careful how we enjoy our liberty in Christ? (p. 55)
   e. What griefs might the Holy Spirit spare us by warning against seeking attention? (p. 58)
   f. Describe a time when God's voice was evidenced by the impact it had on you. (p. 63)
3. Direct participants to complete the viewer guide on page 65 as they watch video session 4 [39:42].
4. Close the session with prayer for experiencing God's character.

❈ SESSION FIVE ❈
God's Voice Reveals His Plan

Before the Session
1. Study week 4 and complete the learning activities. As you study, list questions you plan to ask during the group session. Give special attention to activities that tell participants they will discuss them in their group session.
2. Preview video session 5.

During the Session
1. Greet participants as they arrive. Congratulate group members on their progress through the study. Open with prayer.
2. Refer to your list of questions to discuss as a group; share the page number as you ask each question so members can refer back to their responses. Possible questions include:
   a. How has your obedience fostered experiencing God personally? (p. 68)
   b. What words of condemnation have you struggled with and wondered whether or not they came from God? (p. 70)
   c. In what areas do you tend to operate out of guilt rather than love? (p. 71)
   d. How has the peace of God helped clarify His leading in your life? (reference p. 75)
   e. What personal beliefs have you allowed to override God's truth? (p. 77)
   f. Recall a time when God's word produced change in your life. How did this change bring glory to God? (p. 81)
3. Direct participants to complete the viewer guide on page 83 as they watch video session 5 [40:43].
4. Close with prayer for experiencing God's plans.

❧ SESSION SIX ❧
Responding to God's Voice

Before the Session

1. Study week 5 and complete the learning activities. As you study, list questions to ask during the group session.
2. Preview video session 6.

During the Session

1. Greet participants as they arrive. Congratulate them for their consistent participation. Open with prayer.
2. Refer to your list of questions to discuss as a group; share the page number as you ask each question so members can refer back to their responses. Possible questions include:
   a. What have you learned to help you avoid the trap of proceeding with your own plans and asking God to bless the result? (p. 85)
   b. Describe a time when the circumstances of your life confirmed God's leading and steered you in His direction. (p. 90)
   c. What do God's pre-planned purposes suggest about pressure to rush decisions? (p. 94)
   d. How might the decision to choose a more challenging road make room for God's power to be seen in you? (p. 97)
   e. What gifts has the Lord given you to encourage and edify the church to accomplish His purposes in and through them? (p. 100)
3. Direct participants to complete the viewer guide on page 103 as they watch video session 6 [28:52].
4. Make any plans necessary for a celebration after the group concludes next week. You might meet an extra week for fellowship and planning future Bible studies.
5. Close the session with prayer for continuing to know God, hear God, and obey God.

❧ SESSION SEVEN ❧
Summary

Before the Session

1. Study week 6 and complete the learning activities. Mark questions to ask during the group session.
2. Preview video session 7.

During the Session

1. Greet participants as they arrive. Congratulate group members for completing the study. Open with prayer.
2. Refer to your list of questions to discuss as a group; share the page number as you ask each question so members can refer back to their responses. Possible questions include:
   a. Has God ever asked you to do something that seemed shocking and unreasonable? (p. 105)
   b. How is it difficult to believe God's benefits outweigh the cost of obedience? (p. 108)
   c. What adjustments would you have to make for your plans to align with God's plans right now? (p. 112)
   d. What "ships" is the Lord asking you to burn so you can move forward in committed obedience to Him? (p. 119)
   e. What would you say were the three most important things we have learned together during this study?
3. Watch video session 7 [4:36]. You might want to include the ladies roundtable discussion on DVD 2 here [30:00].
4. Close with prayer for experiencing God's plans.
5. Your group may desire to have a fellowship meal or other celebration. Consider what you may do together to involve others in Bible study and to continue your Bible-study journey.

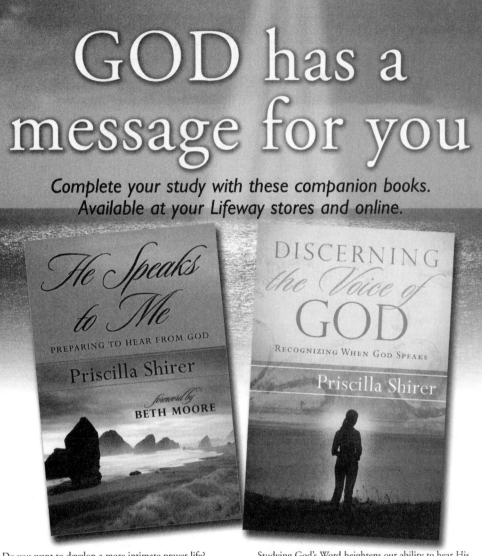

GOD has a message for you

Complete your study with these companion books.
Available at your Lifeway stores and online.

Do you want to develop a more intimate prayer life? More than that, do you want to hear from God in practical ways? Let Priscilla Shirer guide you toward a deeper understanding of the Holy Spirit. **He Speaks to Me** is based on the life of the Old Testament hero, Samuel, who first heard God's voice while still a small boy. By directly meeting our innate need to have a functioning prayer life, **He Speaks to Me** also helps foster a deeper, more meaningful relationship with God.
978-0-8024-5007-4

Studying God's Word heightens our ability to hear His still small voice and it helps us recognize the promptings of the Holy Spirit. Noted author and speaker Priscilla Shirer walks you through Scripture that captures the method and tone of God's communication. She also teaches you how to discern counterfeit voices. God's voice might sound different in various encounters, but the nature of it never changes.
978-0-8024-5009-8

MOODY
PUBLISHERS

THE NAME YOU CAN TRUST®

Two Ways to Earn Credit
for Studying LifeWay Christian Resources Material

CHRISTIAN GROWTH STUDY PLAN

CONTACT INFORMATION:
Christian Growth Study Plan
One LifeWay Plaza, MSN 117
Nashville, TN 37234
CGSP info line 1-800-968-5519
www.lifeway.com/CGSP
To order resources 1-800-485-2772

Christian Growth Study Plan resources are available for course credit for personal growth and church leadership training.

Courses are designed as plans for personal spiritual growth and for training current and future church leaders. To receive credit, complete the book, material, or activity. Respond to the learning activities or attend group sessions, when applicable, and show your work to your pastor, staff member, or church leader. Then go to *www.lifeway.com/CGSP*, or call the toll-free number for instructions for receiving credit and your certificate of completion.

For information about studies in the Christian Growth Study Plan, refer to the current catalog online at the CGSP Web address. This program and certificate are free LifeWay services to you.

Need a CEU?

CONTACT INFORMATION:
CEU Coordinator
One LifeWay Plaza, MSN 150
Nashville, TN 37234
Info line 1-800-968-5519
www.lifeway.com/CEU

Receive Continuing Education Units (CEUs) when you complete group Bible studies by your favorite LifeWay authors.

Some studies are approved by the Association of Christian Schools International (ACSI) for CEU credits. Do you need to renew your Christian school teaching certificate? Gather a group of teachers or neighbors and complete one of the approved studies. Then go to *www.lifeway.com/CEU* to submit a request form or to find a list of ACSI-approved LifeWay studies and conferences. Book studies must be completed in a group setting. Online courses approved for ACSI credit are also noted on the course list. The administrative cost of each CEU certificate is only $10 per course.